Born to Survive

Born to Survive

*The Memoir of a Second World War
Fighter and Test Pilot*

Squadron Leader Allan Scott, DFM

Ellingham Press

British Library Cataloguing in Publication Data

A catalogue record for this book is available from the British Library

ISBN 978-0-9926031-2-0

**Ellingham Press, 43 High Street, Much Wenlock,
Shropshire TF13 6AD**

www.ellinghampress.co.uk

Cover design by Aardvark Illustration and Design

www.aardvarkid.co.uk

Cover painting by Rob Evans
www.restorebike.co.uk

Typesetting by ISB Typesetting, Sheffield

Printed in the UK by Graphics and Print Ltd
www.graphicsandprint.com

Contents

Aircraft Types Flown by S/Ldr Allan Scott

Airspeed
Oxford (t)
Armstrong-Whitworth
Albemarle (t)
Whitley (t)
Avro
Anson (t)
Lancaster (m)
Lincoln (m)

Boeing
B17 Fortress (m)
B29 Washington (m)
Boulton Paul
Defiant (s)
Bristol
Beaufighter (t)
Blenheim (t)
Buckingham (t)
Buckmaster (t)

Cierva
Autogyro
Chance-Vought
Corsair (s)

De Havilland
Chipmunk (s)
Fox Moth (s)
Gypsy Moth (s)
Hornet Moth (s)
Tiger Moth (s)
Vampire (s)
Venom (s)
Devon (t)
Dominie (t)
Dove (t)
Hornet (t)
Mosquito (t)
Heron (m)
Douglas
Boston (t)
Dakota (t)
Havoc (t)

English Electric
Lightning (t)
Canberra (t)

Fairchild
Argus (s)
Fairey
Barracuda (s)

Gloster
Gladiator (s)
Meteor (t)

Handley-Page
Harrow (t)
Halifax (m)
Hastings (m)
Hawker
Hunter (s)
Hurricane (s)
Tempest (s)
Typhoon (s)
Hunting
Jet Provost (s)

Junkers
Ju52 (m)

Lockheed
Hudson (t)

Messerschmitt
Me109 (s)
Mignet
Flying Flea
Miles
Magister (s)
Martinet (s)
Master (s)
Mentor (s)
Monitor (t)

North American
Harvard (s)
Mustang (s)
Mitchell (t)

Percival
Prentice (s)
Proctor (s)
Provost (s)
Vega Gull (s)
Pembroke (t)
Percival Q6 (t)

Republic
Thunderbolt (s)

Scottish Aviation
Twin Pioneer (t)

Taylorcraft
Auster (s)

Vickers
Valetta (t)
Viking (t)
Warwick (t)
Wellington (t)
Vickers-Supermarine
Seafire (s)
Sea Otter (s)
Spitfire (s) Marks 1–9 (Merlin)
Spitfire (s) Mark 14 (Griffon)
Walrus (s)
Vultee
Vengeance (s)

Westland
Lysander (s)

Helicopters
Westland
Wessex
Whirlwind

Other
Glider

(s) single engine
(t) twin engine
(m) multi engine

Acknowledgements

My grateful and sincere thanks go to Alex Madeley for helping me put this story together and to Roy Dolton, President Shropshire Aero Club, for facilitating our venture; also to Martin Bourne for his drawings and help with technical detail and Rob Evans for his front-cover painting.

For additional background information on Malta see *Fortress Malta, An Island Under Siege* by James Holland (Orion 2003).

Preface

I was born a twin in 1921.

Following the influenza pandemic of 1918/1919, my twin sister and I fell ill in another outbreak of flu in the early 1920s. Medical knowledge at the time was unable to combat the virus, and my sister died while I, being the stronger of the two, managed to survive.

For my parents, this was, of course, the tragic loss of their only daughter. For me, from the very beginning of my life, it seemed to mark my future.

It appeared that I was born to survive.

Chapter 1

Joining up with the Royal Air Force

It was nearly every boy's dream then: the sky buzzing with the sound of engines from the de Havilland, Miles and Fairey aircraft factories, newsreels showing off the flying feats of every daring pilot. How could it not be? And many a boy lucky enough to have had a ride in one of Alan Cobham's planes when his Flying Circus came to town would be hooked as soon as the wheels left the ground. So it had been with me. I was about eleven when they flew into Southport and my father booked me a ride in a de Havilland Fox Moth. I have a vivid memory of standing by the pay booth and looking in wonder across the sand at this aircraft, the pilot sitting in the cockpit waving to the attendant to bring the passengers to him, the engine ticking over expectantly.

I could not believe that it was me, that it was really *me* who was following the attendant towards the Moth. My heart thumped all the way. When we reached it, he helped me to climb up to the cabin along a black-looking foot walk made of sandpaper that was attached to the lower wing. My shoes gripped it reassuringly. The cabin struck me as being quite small, perhaps just big enough to hold two adult passengers on the bench seats that faced each other. It reminded me of a much smaller version of a train carriage – and I was to have it all to myself! It seems that in the early 1930s, many were still wary of flying. The fact that a young solitary lad was going up was a bonus to the Circus. It helped promote confidence in the onlookers.

1

The Fox Moth, I was to learn later, was similar to a Tiger Moth in appearance, the only difference being that instead of a seat in front of the pilot, it had a cabin. The pilot had an aperture in the dashboard through which he could check on his passengers and speak to them at any time. I sat on the back seat facing forward and looking out of the window. At Southport, the tide takes the sea a fair distance out, which leaves a large area of perfect flat sand. I saw how this had been made into an airstrip and noticed, too, that there was something hanging on a pole close by. It was a windsock, of course, but I had no knowledge then of what it was for.

Jolted from my thoughts, a voice behind me called, 'Hello, this is the pilot. We're just about to take off!' No sooner said than the aircraft started to move forward, faster, and then faster. I found myself staring at the sand whizzing by in a long strip of what seemed like a dizzying, noisy speed until it came – that incredible, magical feeling of lift. We were in the air, we were *flying*. In no time, my eyes were caught by the sight of the left wing dipping towards the ground. The pilot, I came to realise, was making a gradual turn to the left and there, just as quickly and passing us by, was the Big Dipper in the fairground. I marvelled at the tiny cars climbing up that huge, steep ramp before they hurtled down again and rushed around the bends. Then up came the wing and we were flying level – but not for long. The left wing soon dipped once more and we were heading out towards the sea. That, for me, was the most wonderful, the most exciting sight to behold, but I had only a few moments to take it in before the sand was whizzing by again and I felt a bump. We had landed. I think the whole trip took no more than ten minutes but what could I expect for only half a crown (12½p). As far as I was concerned, it had been worth every single penny. The seed was sown the minute I had stepped into that Moth. I would be a pilot.

But that was not the career I first started. At the age of eighteen and being particularly gifted with the art of drawing, I was recommended to go for architecture as a profession. My aim, if I found that this was to be the career for me, was to take a degree. So I started my initial introduction with Mr Webber, FRIBA, a gentle man amazingly tolerant of a teenager whose only serious thoughts were for joining the RAF and becoming a fighter pilot. My first tasks were to draw accurate plans of proposed new building designs using a drawing pen and black pelican ink for the first time and aiming to draw lines of equal width. With practice and perseverance I soon managed to deliver plans to the satisfaction of Mr Webber. I progressed from this rather boring and mediocre task to actual design, each day having to read and inwardly digest the contents of 'Banister Fletcher', a huge volume of architectural information which soon brought me to the conclusion that this profession was really not for me. My thoughts had begun to turn ever more frequently to flying and the RAF.

And that is how I found myself in early 1940 joining the scores of hopefuls, all with the same intention, eagerly presenting themselves at RAF Padgate, the recruiting centre nearest to me. Most of us were no doubt trying to blank out any doubts that we might not be selected. Fit and ambitious young men think the world's their oyster and too many had been swept off their feet by the inspirational flying of the likes of Sir Alan Cobham and his pilots to ever consider they could not be up there with them. I arrived at Warrington by train from Liverpool and with suitable directions from a local made my way to Padgate's complex of large wooden huts divided into many offices. After some searching, I eventually came across the reception for recruitment and entered. A flight sergeant sitting behind a table in a large office greeted me and I sat down in front of him. He went through the usual personal details including my present occupation and then asked me the inevitable question. Why did I want to join the RAF? I launched enthusiastically into flying and my wanting to become a fighter pilot. This was a big mistake. I was in full flow when he put up his hand to halt me and pointed to a chair across the room where other applicants were waiting to be told, 'You will be called.' We waited. At last, and some time later, I was glad to be invited into another office where I was confronted by the recruiting officer, again sitting behind a table, and once more I was told to take a seat facing him. Apparently, the flight sergeant had informed him of my occupation – a trainee architect – and this was my reason for seeing him. After a short discussion, he told me that architecture was a reserved occupation and that I could not be accepted into the RAF. The disappointment came as a dull shock, and I returned home with a heavy heart.

I was determined that the recruiting officer's words would not put me off. I presented myself for a second time at Padgate, this time telling them that I was a draughtsman (which was part of being an architect) and I was accepted. An enormous wave of relief carried me out of the building.

The RAF at that time was desperate for pilots. Even so, the selection procedure was pretty rigorous. The Board was well known for its accuracy in picking out those best suited to become pilots – bomber or fighter – and those whose role would be in other seats, as observers or air gunners. There was an intense mixture of hope and anxiety in the crowd of young men filing through that awful Board, all of them hungry to be pilots. They would come out of it one by one with their thumbs up or down labelling themselves with their new designation: 'observer', 'air gunner', 'pilot'. I had no intention (at least in my own mind) of becoming anything other than a fighter pilot.

We sat in a waiting room ready to be summoned. A pretty young girl in blue uniform entered and called my name. I acknowledged her and followed her into a long, brightly lit room. Three officers sat on one side of a long table while on the other, facing them, was a single empty chair.

'Please sit down,' one of them said and gestured towards it. In that split second I was reminded, unfortunately, of an interrogation room I had once seen in a film. The memory unsettled me and I sat down nervously. I needn't have worried. The officers were pleasant and reassuring which helped to calm me and to prepare myself to answer their questions. I can't remember much of what they asked but two tests remain vivid. The first was a mental arithmetic sum that was barked at me – 'Multiply 365 by 136!' – *that* took some time to work out, but I managed it eventually with considerable relief. When I turned it over in my mind afterwards, I was glad that I'd stumbled. If my answer had come quickly and correctly, I would have been classed as an 'observer'.

The second test, a book of floral patterns, was handed to me.

'Right, look at the page and tell me what number you see,' the officer instructed.

'Six,' I replied, spotting the number shape at once from among the coloured patterns, and went on to work my way through the book. This was, of course, the colour-blind test and a vital one to establish whether or not potential pilots could differentiate red from green. The runway controller on an airfield could flash a red or green signal on the Aldis lamp or fire a red or green flare from his Very pistol.

The tests completed, I emerged from the Board. I was lucky to be passed but not as a fighter pilot because in the first instance you were just passed for air crew. This could mean ending up as a pilot or an observer or air gunner. Later screening would determine which category you would fall into: fighter or bomber. I felt on top of the world – I felt marvellous! – more than ready to start.

But, of course, all military training must begin with the basic necessities and what better way to bring a hopeful pilot down to earth than to put him through the ITW or Initial Training Wing, the training period for getting us into shape: putting us through lots of drill and discipline, in other words. This was at Newquay, Cornwall where the RAF had requisitioned three of the biggest hotels on one of the fronts facing the beach. The main one, the Trenance, served as the headquarters and also the 'feeding station' as it held the kitchens and dining rooms.

Remembering the kitchens always puts me in mind of 'jankers' or punishments. 'On jankers' was a term then commonly used in the military to mean being put to menial tasks. It was a strange-sounding expression, but it seems the word may have originated in India. The kitchens were a favourite place to put those unfortunates who had fallen foul of the system and been charged. Here the hapless miscreant would have to wade through endless piles of washing-up in the form of mountains of dishes used by the whole squadron. I personally remember this as I was caught, just the once, trying to get back to my hotel after hours. The list of 'jankers' could be endless, but there was another I particularly recall: all-night guard duty at the entrance to the hotels. Some preferred this to the other option, which was taking cold PT sessions on the beaches. Personally, I preferred the PT. It was actually enjoyable, even on bitterly cold mornings and wearing just a pair of gym shorts. After all, these exercises turned us into extremely fit young men.

Fitness was also improved by the regular drill sessions. These were held each morning after breakfast. We would form up in a squad of twelve in front of the hotel waiting for Corporal Jones, the drill corporal, to appear. He was the epitome of his role: extremely smart, the brass buckle on his belt always gleaming with the same brightness, the boots always polished like mirrors and the cane ever present under his arm. He would march us up and down the front, barking out his orders in a pronounced Welsh accent and taking us through the various forms of drill. Often he would lead us around the town and we would march in step with arms swinging shoulder high. This gave us the opportunity to show how smart we were, the white flashes in our hats announcing to the world that we were training air crew. However, as young and budding air crew, our discipline was still very much in its early stages, and we wore poor Corporal Jones ragged. But he took the flak in good humour.

Chapter 2

Initial Training

Those early days soon passed. We grew anxious to get them over, keen to be doing the actual flying. My first rank was sergeant and I was posted to my initial flying training at Woodley in Berkshire, a civil airport with a white control tower. Here I learned to fly in a Magister, a two-seat monoplane with open cockpit built by the Miles Aircraft company for the RAF as a basic trainer. Its low wing was a good introduction to flying Spitfires and here I had a marvellous time.

My first instructor was a tall, quiet man by the name of Flying Officer Frith. It was he who taught me to fly and I managed to go solo in seven hours (the average time was eight) so I felt quite chuffed. At the time, I remember, I was in keen competition with a fellow student called Colin Coulthard; we both did it in seven hours. Later on, I came under another instructor, Flying Officer 'Curly' Dryden. He was an ex-racing driver and as bald as a coot, hence the nickname. What a character! He just aerobatted all over the sky and when he realised my inclination was to become a fighter boy, I was with him all the way. From then on, I was weaned on flinging the aeroplane about and relished every single trip. I began to feel, at last, that I was on the road to reaching my goal.

I flew most of the time with my instructor though I was occasionally tested for my progress and ability by the chief instructor, Squadron Leader Hooper, and was pleased that on each test I passed successfully. But there was one particular flight that is etched on my memory. This was with the commanding officer,

Miles Magister – At the time of the Magister's introduction the first deliveries of Hurricanes and Spitfires were being made, and the new trainer, with its low-wing monoplane characteristics and split trailing-edge flaps, reproduced the handling qualities of these fighters, making the Magister an ideal fighter-pilot trainer.

Wing Commander Moir. He was a formidable character, always dressed in his white flying overalls (I suppose this distinguished him from the instructors). Having been informed that my progress was reported to be above average, he announced that he would give me a final test. We took off and he put me through all aspects of flying, including spinning and aerobatics, which suited me down to the ground. Then out of the blue, a strange aircraft appeared, but not from Woodley. It seemed to have broken the rules of airmanship, which incensed the CO. He set about following the aircraft all the way to the nearby aerodrome of White Waltham where it landed and where we duly followed it in. Having landed ourselves, the Wing Commander stormed into the control room behind the offending pilot. I have no idea who the poor chap was but I bet he got, in RAF vernacular, 'a severe bollocking'. The Wing Commander eventually appeared, returned to the Magister and without another word took off. We headed back to base. All this time I had been sitting in the aircraft watching this going on and keeping quiet. I did not want to be on the wrong side of an irate CO. He was not a man to be trifled with. Personally, I can never understand people who allow their rage to take over in this way. I know one thing for a fact that throughout all my flying, keeping calm helped me to survive through many dangerous incidents.

This period of training lasted twenty-five hours. We were moved next to the more advanced training, this time flying Miles Masters, a faster aeroplane with a Rolls-Royce Kestrel in-line engine. It also had a sideways-opening canopy, the effect of which was to make the pilot feel hemmed in, not a nice feeling at first after the open cockpit of the Magister. In no time, though, we got used to it and began to appreciate the difference in speed, especially approaching to land, and after a few more hours I moved on to my first night flying. For the initial few circuits, I was taken up dual so as to get used to using instruments for the first time and to be shown how different it was to land an aircraft at night. After that, and having taxied back to dispersal, the instructor climbed out, put his thumb up and shouted, 'Off you go – solo!' The dim lighting made taxiing out difficult, but I got to the end of the runway and with a 'green' from the controller, I turned on to the runway itself. This was illuminated with goose-neck flares which were not the brightest of lighting, and trying to read instruments in the pitch black was quite a shaky experience. I opened up the throttle rolling forward, keeping it straight on the left goose-necks and took off, climbing into the blackness, but I was sweating. I had to look at those bloody instruments! At 1,000 feet, I levelled out and turned onto a downwind heading. All was well up to then. I looked left to see if I could pick out the runway, but it was a struggle to make out those goose-neck flares. I did manage it at last and here I have to confess to cheating. With the runway in sight, I did a visual circuit and landed. However, I persevered with further landings and take-offs and learned to stay on instruments, and to trust them. I finished this part of the training and after another twenty-five hours heard that I was to fly Hurricanes.

At that time Spitfires were only just being introduced, so the Hurricane, the main fighter in the war by then, was the first fighter I flew. Although heavy and solid, I found them a really good aircraft to fly, an exceptionally stable gun platform. But I was not long on them, being soon transferred to the Spitfire – and it was the Spitfire that was to become my real joy. I called them a grown-up Tiger Moth, with no vices. Some pilots found them difficult to land, with their narrow undercarriage but I discovered that by levelling it out over the runway at the correct height, waiting until it was about to stall, then pulling the stick back to my stomach, it would land perfectly on three points. To fly this aircraft, you became a part of it. Sitting on the seat, it fitted like a glove, the side walls conforming to your shoulders, the controls at your fingertips and obeying every command at a touch, so that you never had to think about working it. In combat, with a turn of the head and the eyes, it would follow that direction without deviation; upside down and you were held in your seat, as though glued to it. All these qualities proved to be so valuable in combat, especially in a dogfight when the easy flow of vital manoeuvres meant the difference between life and death. It was a truly incredible aircraft and the number of times the Spitfire saved my life was equally astonishing. I may have been born to survive, but this machine played a vital part in it.

Chapter 3

My First Squadron

Not long to go, I kept reassuring myself, just a few more hours and we'd be ready for battle – well, not quite. I had, by now, only about fifty or sixty hours' flying under my belt. Although the hectic, knife-edge days of the Battle of Britain had officially drawn to a close in October 1940, actual raids of German bombers on Britain continued until December 1941. It was during this period that I had the great fortune to be posted to 124 Squadron at Biggin Hill. Biggin Hill, south-east of London, was of course one of the most famous of RAF aerodromes and played a key role in the Battle, its objective to protect the south-east and the approaches to the capital. But as it happened, in September 1941 and not long after my posting there, the entire squadron was moved for a period of rest to Castletown in Caithness, northern Scotland. This turned out to be lucky for me in a way because it gave me a few more hours flying on Spitfires and, more importantly, the experience of dogfighting. Up in the Highlands we had the airspace completely to ourselves, which meant we had the best opportunity to practise all the tactics required for operational flying. It was an extremely useful introduction.

But amidst all the flying practice there was time for leisure. A group of us would sometimes travel in a squadron truck into Thurso, the nearest town to the camp. Here, tucked among the line of stone cottages that edged the wide main street and built of the same rugged stone, was the local cinema. It had progressed little through the Thirties and the films they showed

11

were all black and white and silent. The projectionist had to crank the handle to turn the reel and the clickety-clack noise in that small room was deafening. The uproarious comments this provoked from the pilots were hilarious and met with unamused stares from the locals who thought we were completely mad. Of course, to us, the whole show was a hoot.

The rest period came to an abrupt end in November 1941 and the squadron was moved back to Biggin Hill. This would be the beginning of my initiation to operational flying and my meeting, at last, with the enemy – the Luftwaffe. Fortunately for us, young eager pilots that we were, there was still bags of enemy action to contend with, of that we were certain. The squadron commander was Squadron Leader Duke-Woolley and Flight Lieutenants Barton and Tommy Balmforth were flight commanders. It was a wonderful squadron to be a part of, its spirit and companionship were terrific and it was very much an international unit. There was Bob Larcher from Mauritius, Coul from Poland – or perhaps it was Czechoslovakia – Bertie the Belgian, two pilots from Norway, two from Canada and one Free French who had a small dachshund called Zi-Zi. It was like the Tower of Babel at times, though everybody was obliged to speak English. Occasionally in a dogfight, excitement would get the better of them and some would bellow in their mother tongue, which was only natural. But if a 'mike' was left switched on we were in trouble. On one occasion Canuck the Canadian gave an unintentional but very exciting commentary on his activities, much to the delight and entertainment of the WAAF in the operation room.

When we were scrambled there were twelve aircraft per squadron and in the early days we flew in a line-astern formation. It was later that we changed and flew in line-abreast against the enemy. With line-astern, the fourth aircraft in each line was the look-out and was known as 'arse-end charlie'. This was the most dangerous position to fly. However, if you weaved enough, used your eyes and reported any enemy diving down on the formation, you saved many a bounce. But the truth was, if you had no battle experience, as of course none of us did in those early days, you didn't see anything; the

First Squadron – 124
Back Row L–R: Coul, Bob Larcher
Middle Row: Penny, Timber Woods, Mike Reid, Tommy Balmforth,
Sqn Ldr Duke-Woolley, Slim Kilburn, Canuck, myself, Kothera
Front Row: Bertie the Belgian, Foxy, Jessie Hibberd, a Norwegian
pilot, Grandpa, another Norwegian pilot, Johnny Hull.

leader could be heard reporting, '25 plus 8 o'clock...', '40 plus
to your right 3 o'clock coming out of the sun...', but no matter
how much you strained, eyeballs out like chapel hat-pegs, you
could not see them. This was when we relied upon our leader's
experience and sight to get us through, weaving all the harder
and following him blindly. We flew in sheer terror half the
time and obviously there were losses; the list grew in one week
alone: Mike, Penny and Coul on the same day in April, Eddie
on the twenty-fourth, Badge and Fuey on the twenty-fifth, Bob
and Kothera on the twenty-seventh and lastly, Grandpa on the
thirtieth. But war, sadly, cannot stop for its casualties. We had
to get on with the job.

There were good days to offset the bad and keep our spirits
high. A visit by King George VI to Biggin Hill was the highlight
of one week. The squadron lined up dressed in flying kit ready
to go on a sweep over the Channel to France and each pilot was

A Flight
L-R: Bertie the Belgian, Bob Larcher, Jessie Hibberd, Slim Kilburn,
Coul, myself, Canuck the Canadian, a Norwegian pilot.

Myself shaking hands with King George VI during his visit to
Biggin Hill.

introduced to him by Squadron Leader Duke-Woolley. I was delighted to get a shot of me shaking hands with His Majesty taken by the camp photographer.

I had the good fortune around this time to fly with Wing Commander Tuck (Robert Stanford Tuck) as his number two. He was already an ace, credited with more than thirty kills. I followed him blindly at first and learnt a lot from his experience so that, at nineteen, I suddenly found myself, adrenalin flowing, coming up the tail of the Luftwaffe's twin-engine, multi-role Junkers 88 (Ju88), firing at it and wondering how the hell I had got there. That was my first kill and there was no doubt about it; it was thrilling to down an enemy aircraft. This feeling increased with my catching sight, while still weaving madly to check for more Messerschmitt 109 fighters, that the German crew had baled out.

The days passed quickly and my experience grew. I got better at spotting aircraft in the sky. Now, when the leader reported '20 plus 7 o'clock', my head would turn round and my eyes would pick them out clearly. It was good to feel a useful part of the squadron and to join in the many dogfights with the Me109s. Of course, it was frightening. Cold sweat would run down my face but the adrenalin never stopped, nor did the thrill. In the comfortable light of peacetime it seems a hard thing to say that you thoroughly enjoyed the war. But as fighter pilots our main concern was to knock enemy aircraft out of the sky and there was always the chance, if the aircraft had not been destroyed, that the crew could bale out.

Returning home could be primitive. In these early days there were no such refinements as air traffic. Air traffic control consisted then of a single airman manning a caravan at the end of the direction to land (there were no runways at Biggin Hill, it was a grass airfield). He would have a Very pistol and an Aldis lamp and would flash a red on the lamp or set off a red with the gun if you hadn't thought about putting the undercarriage down. Our navigation could be a bit hairy too and returning to base after a dogfight it was easy to get disorientated, particularly over the Channel. In that case, if we put the sun in our back we knew we would be heading north and not to the

French coast. The white cliffs would appear, we would cross the coast and, still heading north, continue flying until we saw the straight railway line from Ashford to Redhill, then turn left and keep flying along it until a 'V' junction appeared. Here we would turn right and fly up that rail until some working sandpits came into view and then it was over them to Biggin Hill ahead. If the weather was bad, it was the same procedure only at zero feet. This sort of navigation raised the question of why not use a compass. Well, sometimes it was toppled and, in some unfortunate cases, shot away. The instruments, in any case, were basic to say the least.

There were occasions when the squadron was stood down. This was good because it meant a break from combat, sometimes for a few hours, sometimes for as long as a day. At these times, the pilots would depart en masse into Bromley, which was the nearest town to Biggin Hill, or go off to the swimming baths to do dinghy drill (this meant taking over the place and dinghy drill soon became something hilarious to us). We seemed to find most things hilarious, come to think of it. Perhaps it was because of the kind of life we were living; after all, a fighter pilot's life in combat was estimated at only fifteen minutes. 'Live for today, tomorrow may never come' was the motto.

Of course dinghy drill was extremely important. Any of us could find ourselves in the unfortunate position of having to bale out over the Channel, plunging into the cold sea. The drill was to get us practised at inflating the dinghy and pulling ourselves into it as soon as possible. This latter was not an easy thing to do. We had to position ourselves face down, slide the dinghy under our stomachs and kick our legs to get a bit of propulsion (difficult to do with heavy flying boots on). Usually at this stage it would roll sideways, plunging us back into the water. The hoots of laughter and flow of derisive remarks would make many a dull practice into an enjoyable outing. But it also made sure it was instilled into our memory for good.

Also in Bromley was the country club, a place well patronised by us. One evening in a typical 'letting off steam' prank, Jessie H climbed under the table and behind the cloth, completely hiding himself from the rest of us. From this interesting position, he was shouting out at the top of his voice, the boys sitting around the table joining in the fun and not letting on where the voice was coming from. The whole place erupted, a quiet, genteel country club no more. Usually we would walk back to base (some would have had a few 'sherbets' too many), and Jessie would perform another of his pranks. This time, he would stop in the middle of the road and put his thumb up in the hitch-a-lift sign. With petrol rationing, there were very few cars around then; traffic was a rarity. However, this did not deter Jessie. He would stand on the edge of the road thumbing to an imaginary car which would make an imaginary stop. He would open the imaginary door and say to the boys, 'We've got a lift. Pile in!' and there we would be, sitting in the middle of the road, not a car in sight and much to the amusement of any passers-by. Stupid, yes – but we were young, eighteen, nineteen, twenty perhaps.

Chapter 4

Posted to Malta

Joining up in 1940, I would never have imagined that an island more or less the size of the Isle of Wight would be the scene of some of the most intense and thrilling action I would experience during the war. Yet by 1942 the mere thought of Malta was to get the adrenalin going.

The Italians had been the first to lay siege to it in 1940, joined later by the Germans; relentless attacks by their navies and air forces had rendered this tiny island in dire need of rescue. Malta was to become known as the most bombed place on earth. The reason was its position, long recognised as strategically important for any nation with imperial interests in the region and beyond. In the early years of the nineteenth century Nelson had acknowledged its importance in gaining control of the Mediterranean, and when, in 1814, Malta itself sought our protection from the French, its annexation to the Crown gave Britain that very advantage, enhanced by the fact that it lay almost exactly between Gibraltar (another British territory) at the western mouth of the Mediterranean and Suez at the eastern end. During WWII Malta's importance was no less significant. This small piece of land was to become a base from which to protect British interests from Axis attacks in the Middle East, Egypt, India and the Far East. But getting there was tough. Flying on transport aircraft was impossible. The constant bombing and strafing by fighter aircraft meant that the risk of being shot down either on approaching the island, or if you were lucky enough to get that far, on landing was too high.

So there was only one approach and that was by sea. I joined the *Empire Darwin* in Milford Haven harbour, an American vessel sent as part of the lease-lend agreement. Its orders were to join a five-knot convoy, five knots being the slowest of the ships in the convoy. We were welcomed aboard by the merchant seamen and shown to our quarters, a hold converted into a leisure room and sleeping quarters. This was where we would be living for the next ten days. It was comfortable enough, and there was easy access to the main deck above, as long as you got the hang of climbing almost vertical steel ladders. Coming down them was much easier, of course – providing you held on to the side rails, a good slide would get you from top to bottom in an instant. We were given the freedom to roam around and explore the ship, which most of us were glad to do. So we set sail in early July from Milford Haven to Bangor in Northern Ireland where the complete convoy was formed. From there the course was set: around the north coast of Ireland, into the Atlantic and down to Gibraltar.

It was an interesting voyage. At one point I got talking to one of the crew, a 'grease monkey' I think he was called. I asked him what exactly his job was. He told me that he had to grease the propeller shaft and invited me to accompany him down to the shaft, to see it working. I followed him down a vertical ladder into the bowels of the ship and into a tunnel. We crawled along this tunnel, a shiny steel revolving propeller shaft alongside us, until he stopped at what looked like a square box fitted over the spinning shaft. Here he promptly poured oil or grease into the box. There were several boxes like this at intervals along the full length of the shaft but one box was enough for me. I think I was already crawling my way back along the tunnel, desperate for fresh air, when he caught up with me. But he understood. As if the smell and the tight space were not enough, the thought had also occurred to me that it would be a very dicey part of the ship to be in if a U-boat should attack. I don't consider myself even now to be claustrophobic but I knew then that I would never volunteer to do a stunt like that again! By complete contrast, on another occasion, I made friends with the first mate and was invited to the bridge, something I really appreciated. Life on board was generally very interesting.

There were downsides, of course. The crew had informed us (the RAF rookies) that the ship was of an all-welded steel construction with no rivets and, with only the speed of five knots in a storm, there was no give. The ride was rough, as we were to find out. In mid Atlantic one night the ship was involved in a force 10 gale with waves sixty feet high which, on one occasion, swept completely over it. We pilots, trying to sleep, didn't know whether we were upside down or not. It was a very long night indeed. In the morning, getting to breakfast proved an interesting trip. The ship was still in the storm and rolling quite a bit, so to make our way to the galley we were tied in turn on an endless rope and hauled along the deck. Being unhitched at the galley end was a disaster, as on the first roll I lost my feet and slid painfully on the steel deck to the far end. Under guidance, I was able to wedge myself to stop further sliding. Bruised but otherwise all right, I reached the breakfast end at last where I was fascinated to see the large cauldrons that were slung on hooks. Managing to keep steady, the cook scooped great spoonfuls of food from them with considerable skill when the ship was in the middle of a roll.

Another interesting feature of this ship was that it was rigged with a Hurricane on a catapult on the bow. The storm had not been kind to it and it was waterlogged. The ship's crew worked hard to get it serviceable. It was there to engage German reconnaissance planes, the long-distance four-engine Focke-Wulf Condors that might come across our convoy. The snag with this was that after the engagement the Hurricane had to ditch or the pilot bale out. Ditching was the preferred option, as the parachute was vulnerable in very strong winds, a very unpleasant thought if Gibraltar was not in range. I was thankful that I was not the pilot for this task, but we were lucky on this trip: there were no U-boat attacks and no Condor for the Hurricane to deal with. Our sea voyage was actually enjoyable and we arrived in Gibraltar in mid July 1942.

Chapter 5

Carrier HMS Eagle

As we disembarked from the *Empire Darwin*, Gibraltar was an amazing sight to new eyes. Its huge rock towered above us for the whole length of our walk from the docks to the block of rooms that was to be our accommodation until the next leg to Malta. All the pilots were housed here and each had his own room. This was a huge improvement on the steel deck of the hold that had been my bed for too long. But my first taste of luxury was to come in the form of a deep, deep bath, slipping into water that covered me as I lay the full length. Back home in England we had been rationed to six inches of water maximum. Here in Gibraltar the baths were filled with seawater and we were issued with special soap to use in them.

Having settled in, a few of us decided to walk into the town which, in 1942, consisted of one large main street with shops and saloon bars on either side. Again, the contrast to the shops back home with their dull displays and meagre stocks could not have been greater. Here they were ablaze with lights and filled with cigarettes and goods of every kind, although to this day I have never seen so many tobacconists in one street. As we knew there were no cigarettes to be had on Malta, everyone rushed in to buy as many as they could to squeeze into their Spit – and they were cheap: 200 for five old shillings (25p). Of course, we bought a huge quantity, restricted only by what we could carry!

The bars and saloons were large, open places with swing doors opening out on to the street. Every now and then a drunken sailor would appear between the doors and sink to the ground, totally oblivious to what was going on around him and there he would stay until the naval police picket wagon would arrive, sling him in and drive along to the next bar to pick up others. The saloons were crowded and, passing one, I caught the sound of music filtering out on to the street. While we stood there listening, a fight started and it really was a humdinger. Bottles were flying, tables and chairs shot through the doors and, in the midst of it all, the band's piano player carried on playing, expertly ducking the bottles one after the other. It was an incredible sight, like something out of a cowboy film but here, amazingly, in the flesh. The band seemed to be made up mainly of Spanish women. The shopkeepers on the other hand were Spanish men and at curfew time would close their shops and head for the border to cross over to the Spanish side and the nearest town, La Línea. The curfew was always strictly adhered to.

We decided to take a look at that border and get a view of Spain which was, of course, neutral during the war. We walked across the runway, a shortened version of what it is today, and because it really was so close we could see La Línea quite easily. There were German officers sitting in the bars and restaurants and getting close-ups of our side through binoculars. We were very tempted to wave. It amused us to guess what they might be reporting to the Third Reich that time.

But the sightseeing and the luxury baths were soon over. Our quarters awaited us; in the morning we would have to board the *Eagle*. The war was not going to wait.

At Gibraltar, our orders were to fly to Malta a contingent of thirty-six Spitfires off the carrier, HMS *Eagle*. This was to be the second contingent, the first having already flown off the American carrier *Wasp* in April 1942. Previous to this, the island had been defended initially by three Gladiators known as Faith, Hope and Charity. They had faced tremendous odds and, despite putting up a gallant fight, were getting nowhere. The Hurricanes were then called to take over the defence and, again, while fighting with great courage, their pilots had found

HMS Eagle.

it hard to contain the constant air attacks. The Spitfires had been the next to be sent out but constant losses among these resulted in the despatch of the second contingent to replenish and make up the numbers.

As complete novices, life on a carrier was quite an experience. We were housed in makeshift quarters in a large hangar below decks. I found sleeping in a hammock impossible and had to contend with the hard steel deck as a mattress. Finding the toilet – known as the 'heads' – was also a bit daunting as it meant meandering through a mass of corridors. The sailors were good and helped us and managed, somehow, not to take the mickey.

The Spitfires were loaded, and we pilots made ready. The carrier was to take us a thousand miles down the Mediterranean before we were due to take off. A thousand miles seemed quite a long way. The aircraft had been fitted with long-range tanks which, when empty, would be jettisoned three hours' flying time from Malta. The *Eagle* had been an old merchant ship converted to a carrier and had a pointed bow, not like the later carriers which had square ends and off-set decks. When it was time to take off, the ship would turn into the wind but only stay on this course for as long as it took the first twelve Spitfires to get away, cracking along at about twenty-nine knots which gave us the ground speed of twenty-nine knots plus the wind speed at the time. Then flying would stop and the carrier would start tacking port and starboard to avoid U-boat attacks. This was quite frightening to those of us sitting in our aircraft on the end of the ship, the vessel heeling alarmingly so that you could see the sea over the wing as though banking in a steep turn. The *Eagle* would return to a steady course, then the next twelve would get airborne, and so on.

The Spitfire, beautiful aircraft that it was, did have the disadvantage of a very long nose so that sitting in the cockpit the pilot was not able to see straight ahead when the tail was on the ground. So to assist our take-off, three parallel white lines fore and aft had been painted down the length of the deck. The outer lines could be lined up under the cannons and the centre line to the undercarriage giving the full distance to the end of the bow, though you only got to see this when the Spit was in the level flying position. To aid the take-off, fifteen degrees of flap would have been a help. However, the flaps on the Spitfire operated either fully down or fully up, so good old British improvisation came to the rescue in the form of wooden cheese blocks cut to an angle of fifteen degrees. When we were ready for take-off at the end of the runway, we put the flaps down and a crewman would put the blocks in. Raising the flaps then meant they were held at the crucial fifteen degrees.

We were RAF pilots, of course, not naval pilots and had never taken off from a carrier. Positioned at the end of the runway, with engines running and holding with brakes on, we kept our eyes fixed at 'bats' (the naval crewman with batons). He would be circling his baton indicating for us to open up the throttle and would keep this up until, with his experience, he knew exactly when you had enough revs to wave your take-off run. When it was my turn I was convinced the nose of the Spit would hit the deck but blindly kept opening the throttle until, on his wave forward, I took the brakes off and started my run putting the throttle to fully open. Looking at the left white line under the cannon to hold me straight, I soon came up level and followed the centre line until, at last and gratefully, I was airborne and staggering over the bow. Once airborne the flaps were lowered and the cheese blocks fell away. With flaps raised again, the aircraft was clean and ready to fly towards the formation.

Unfortunately not all take-offs were successful. One pilot must have lost his nerve and failed to open the throttle for full power. He foundered and fell off the bow. Perhaps unnerved at seeing that aircraft go over, the second failure got halfway down the runway, closed his throttle and braked too fast, so with a hard right rudder he turned right and wrapped himself around a Bofors gun, much to the displeasure of the sailors manning it. They had to jump for their lives into the sea. The aircraft was pushed overboard and the pilot, an Australian, was greatly upset – not by what had happened but by the loss of a horde of cigarettes he had carefully stashed behind his seat.

Climbing away from the *Eagle* up to the formation, and having dropped the cheese blocks, we got together and set course for Malta. It was not all plain sailing, or should I say, flying. About halfway, and to the right of our flight path, was the island of Pantelleria. On it was based a squadron of Me109s. We had only enough fuel to fly to Malta and could not afford to get into a dogfight. It was a long, anxious moment or two creeping past that island, tense and sweating. Fortunately there was no radar in those days and we made it. We continued our flight and reached Malta, only to discover that the island was in the middle of an air raid and that we were joining to find Me109s attacking the very airfield we were supposed to land on.

Short of fuel, desperate to land and with a 109 on my tail, there was no time to put the undercarriage up. I heaved the Spit into the tightest turn I have ever made in my life, the adrenalin gripping my body and helping me to evade his attack. He missed. I was able to out-turn him and shake him off. Only then could I attempt another landing. I managed it, aiming towards a pen, parked hurriedly, climbed out and dashed into the slit trench for safety. I was amazed to turn and see my Spit already being refuelled by a string of men – army, navy and air force – who were passing tins of petrol from hand to hand and then up to the 'erk' (aircraftman in RAF slang) who was straddling the fuselage as though on horseback. Desperate to get the aircraft ready for the next scramble, he was pouring the petrol into a large funnel to fill the fuselage tank. I had landed at Takali airfield on 21 July 1942 and had joined 603 Squadron. It was a case of 'welcome to Malta'!

We were at Takali for only a few days before 603 was disbanded and the new 1435 Squadron was formed, based at Luqa. I was transferred to that for the rest of my Malta tour.

Chapter 6

The George Cross Island

Just sixty miles or so from Malta, Sicily had squadrons from the Italian Air Force as well as the Luftwaffe. Malta had been under constant air raid from these for the previous twenty-three months, defended firstly by the Gladiators and then the Hurricanes. By the time we arrived the island had suffered massively and was practically on its knees. With their almost total air superiority, the attacks by the Axis powers had been relentless. The Maltese people suffered incredibly under these raids and lacked everything. They had been bombed out of their homes, had very little fuel, food or clothing and lived with the constant threat of invasion. Moreover, the air raids on them had become vicious, their purpose to crush the spirit of the islanders who had held out for so long. The award of the George Cross during the siege was a fitting recognition of their endurance.

When the second contingent of Spitfires arrived, the pressure from the Axis squadrons increased so that there would be two or three air raids in a day. The principal targets were Grand Harbour (Valletta) and the three airfields of Luqa, Takali and Hal Far.

We were scrambled every day to engage the bombers and escorting 109s as they approached from Sicily and there were many dogfights in the early months of July and August. A couple of examples, one on July 23 and another on August 29, provide a typical picture. On July 23 our squadron was scrambled to intercept a large number of bombers escorted by fighters who were, by the time we got airborne, almost over Malta.

27

Unusually, the island was covered by a white cloud cover and we were able to see the bombers clearly. The first section of our fighters dived down and engaged the bombers while we, the second section of four, were just about to follow when we were attacked by Italian Reggiane fighters and Me109s. A running dogfight started. In a split second the sky was filled with weaving and turning aircraft. I managed to get on the tail of a Reggiane but at first could not fix my gun sights on him as he violently manoeuvred to avoid me. But as he broke to dive and turn for home I did manage to let fly a quick burst of cannon shells and may have damaged him, but did not claim. In the 29 August incident, we were scrambled and climbed quickly to 20,000 feet. There were no bombers this time but a full squadron of Me109s which we engaged. A colossal dogfight followed and again the sky was filled with a confusion of turning aircraft. Near misses were commonplace and it was difficult to make out which aircraft to engage in those split seconds. I did manage to get a 109 this time and saw the cannon shells explode in the engine. He went into the sea. A new tactic by the Luftwaffe then emerged whereby a squadron of Italian fighters would fly with the bombers at 20,000 feet while the Me109s would be above them at 30,000 feet. The scrambled Spitfires would, of course, engage the escorting Italian fighters in order to get at the bombers. Less experienced pilots concentrating on a target would not see the 109s diving out of the sun to sit behind them – with deadly results. Needless to say, our losses were grim, and other tactics became necessary to protect the few aircraft that remained to us.

With such losses, it was normal for our squadron when engaging to be considerably outnumbered by the 109s, usually by about five to one but on occasions when only four of the squadron engaged, it could be as high as twenty to one. My experience taught me that the Germans were immaculately disciplined and would go through hell and high water to follow an order from their leader but they did have to have leadership. German courage was never in question, nor was the British, but ours was very different. Being an island race, it seemed to me, perhaps every man was an individual in his own right, and was prepared to be a leader if the circumstances demanded.

This was highlighted when engaging the bombers. We would target the leading box to destroy its leader. If this was successful the whole fleet, lost without orders, could suddenly turn about or end up in such disarray they were much easier to shoot down. Also, at the times when we had only four Spitfires serviceable to be scrambled, they might be led by a sergeant pilot and on such occasions we would adopt four different call signs – Blue One, Red One, Yellow One and Green One – so that the German listening service would report four squadrons of Spitfires airborne.

Dogfights often ensued when we were bounced by the escorting 109s, but our squadron strategy now, with aircraft so short, was to dive down on the bombers, destroy what we could and then drop to sea level to get back to Malta without loss. We could not afford to lose a single machine. However, the 109s soon got wise to this and would follow us down, with the inevitable dogfight ensuing. I was caught twice this way. On the first occasion I had shot down a Ju88 and dived down to sea level to return to base. By this time our trick of making ourselves out to be four squadrons had been picked up by the German 'Y' service (intelligence gathered from listening into our broadcasts) and passed on to them. Unfortunately, two 109s spotted me and dived down to attack. I saw them coming and out-turned them. A dogfight followed. Making tight turns, I managed to sit on the tail of one of them and, with a quick burst, bagged him. He went into the sea. The other 109 was by this time getting short of fuel and turned for Sicily. I was clear to return to Malta.

The same thing happened on the second occasion. I had got down to sea level and, as usual after a dogfight, was returning to Malta on my own with my ammunition exhausted. I had previously engaged and shot down a Ju88. Again, a dogfight ensued, this time with two Me109s, only this time I was sitting on the tail of one of them and unable to shoot. The German pilots realised this. All I could do was to use the Spitfire in its defensive role and keep out-turning them as they came down. After several tight turns of getting nowhere, they decided it was stalemate. To my utter amazement they came in and, at a reasonable distance, formated on me, waggled their wings and

YEAR 1942		AIRCRAFT		PILOT, OR	2ND PILOT, PUPIL	DUTY
MONTH	DATE	Type	No.	1ST PILOT	OR PASSENGER	(INCLUDING RESULTS AND...)
—		—		—	—	—— TOTALS BROUGHT
AUG	5	SPITFIRE	D.Vb	SELF	—	SCRAMBLE ~. CLIM... UP TO 23,000. R/T... HALF ROLL OUT & AILE... DOWN TO THE DECK.
AUG	9.	SPITFIRE	B.Vb	SELF	—	SCRAMBLE ~. CLIMBE... 26,000 AND GOT SEVE... BOUNCED BY 10 109s. ... THREE OF US JUST HALF... DID AILERON TURNS DOWN... AFTER THAT SHAKY DO. ... A 109 ON MY TAIL Poo... MADLY. OUTURNED HIM... A GOOD SQUIRT IN.
					1. DAMAGED.	
AUG	11.	SPITFIRE	D.Vb	SELF	—	SCRAMBLE ~ CLIMBED... FOLLOWING SOME 109's A... BUT DID NOT ENGAGE.
"	12	SPITFIRE	B.Vb	SELF	—	SCRAMBLE ~. 20,000 f... 12 109's. DID NOT ENG...
" "	13	SPITFIRE	W.Vb	SELF	—	MALTA CONVOY PAT... NO RAID ON OUR SH...
" "	13	SPITFIRE	H.Vb	SELF	—	MALTA CONVOY PAT... RAID CAME IN. WITH BR... 6 109's & SOME REGGIES. ... BLEW UP BREDA §§. WHEN ... BURST IN HIS PETROL TAN... MASS OF FLAME. IT WENT... INTO SEA. NO SURVIVORS
					ONE BREDA DESTROYED.	
GRAND TOTAL [Cols. (1) to (10)]				367 Hrs. 35 Mins.		TOTALS CARRIED

Logbook entry – bombers approaching Malta.

turned for home – Sicily. Obviously, they were running short of fuel. For that brief moment we were no longer enemies but fellow aviators. I often found that the Luftwaffe pilots had the same outlook as our own; of course we were at war and our task was to destroy enemy aircraft, but as far as I was concerned, I was shooting at the aircraft; the pilot could bale out.

As our losses grew, so did the concern at the Air Ministry. In looking at ways they might be reduced, one ministry boffin came up with an 'interesting' thought – that the rays from the sun shining on our new 'perspex bubble hoods' were causing refraction of light and thus preventing pilots from seeing the 'Hun in the sun' diving down on our tails. The Ministry had obviously forgotten, or were unaware, that most of the replacement pilots to the squadron were straight from OTU flying and, as explained earlier, were unable to see the enemy aircraft being reported. The order duly came direct from them to remove all hoods. We had an open cockpit in a 450 mph fighter and at 36,000 feet. This was no joke. I had to lean forward towards the gunsight to try and get the freezing air past me. I and other pilots ended up with completely stiff necks and were rushed into Bighi Naval Hospital for emergency treatment. This was at a time when there were so few of us; pilots could not be spared from operational flying. Even so, it took two days to free our necks sufficiently to return to the squadron and still I was unable to get my neck in the six o'clock position, a major disadvantage for seeing an aircraft on my tail. Fortunately, the hot sun soon helped to ease more flexibility into it, and I was very shortly back to normal. Needless to say, the bubble hoods were replaced the next day.

We had our troubles on the ground as well, with sabotage by a few Italian and Fascist sympathisers. A variety of incidents were brought to light: barbed wire buried in front of the dispersal pens to puncture the tyres taxiing out; a pilot baling out to find, to his horror, a blanket unfolding instead of silk. Such cases caused outrage and fury among the pilots. As a warning of the action that would be taken if anybody was found guilty of sabotage, a gibbet was erected on the airfield. It became a morning drill to check the parachutes by dipping our hand into the pack to make sure that it was silk and not a blanket. The gibbet proved a sufficient deterrent. Nobody was hanged.

Not being able to get my neck to the six o'clock position reminds me of an amusing incident. We would fly during the daytime and each evening we would be taken by bus to the sergeants' mess in St Julian's Bay, near Sliema. After a full day of combat flying we would arrive so exhausted that it took little time for us to fall asleep, in spite of the fact that an anti-aircraft gun emplacement was situated nearby and would fire

most of the night. The bedroom was large with a highly polished wooden floor. Four iron truckle beds stood in it, each one
fitted with a mosquito net attached to the ceiling. Apparently,
it was unusual for an island to have mosquitoes, but they were
in profusion here. We came to realise just how remarkably
alert the subconscious mind could be when, in spite of being
fast asleep, one of the pilots would shout 'six o'clock!' and all

EXTRACT :- D.R.O's DATED 14.5.42
R.A.F. STATION, TA-KALI, MALTA

A GIBBET HAS BEEN ERECTED
ON THE CORNER OF THE ROAD
LEADING TO THE CAVES. ANY
MAN, WOMAN OR CHILD, CIVILIAN
OR SERVICE PERSONNEL, FOUND
GUILTY OF SABOTAGE, THEFT,
OR IN ANY OTHER WAY IMPEDING
THE WAR EFFORT AND SUB-
SEQUENTLY SHOT, WILL BE
HUNG FROM THIS GIBBET AS
A WARNING TO ALL OTHERS.

The gibbet.

of the other three would turn their bodies valiantly within the bed, making the beds slide across the polished floor, pulling the nets with them. We would haul ourselves back by grabbing on to the nets. With the morning came the all too familiar awareness of a very meagre breakfast: a cup of tea and one slice of bread. Then it was back on the bus to dispersal.

The conditions on Malta during these hectic months were grim. As our insubstantial breakfast showed there was little food, not only for the Maltese civilians but for pilots flying every day in combat. I remember being given two ship's biscuits that were too hard to even bite. The cook had the bright idea of soaking all the biscuits in a pail of water. He then cooked the soggy mass into a pudding which was much appreciated and did ease the hunger a little. I lost four stone in weight over a period of six months and, like so many others, had to contend with flying while trying to ignore the demands of the infamous Malta Dog, an appropriate name for violent diarrhoea. Time, like food, was precious. When we were not in the air we would grab what rest we could by sheltering from the blazing sun under the wings of our aircraft, ready to scramble at a second's notice. When in the air, we had to face not only a fierce, relentless enemy but the inhospitable environment of Malta itself. The options for making an emergency landing were dire: either ditching in the sea and hoping to be picked up, or risking a landing in the rocky terrain of fields whose boundaries, unlike the more forgiving hedges back home, were marked by stone walls. It would be a case of straining every hope, every physical effort and what might be left of an aircraft's flying capability to get back to base.

Efforts were continuously being made to keep the island supplied with essentials. This included the use of two submarines, the *Clyde* and the *Porpoise*, which carried three-quarters of their load as fuel to keep the Spitfires airborne, and a quarter as food. Two cruisers, one of them the *Manxman*, also brought food and fuel (their armour had been removed to give them extra speed to outrun the U-boats). This, of course, was insufficient to keep the island alive. A large convoy was essential. Back in the UK, preparations were being made. At various

SINGLE-ENGINE AIRCRAFT			MULTI-ENGINE AIRCRAFT							PASS-ENGER	INSTR./CLOUD FLYING (Incl. in cols. (1) to (10))	
DAY	NIGHT		DAY			NIGHT					DUAL	PILOT
PILOT	DUAL	PILOT	DUAL	1ST PILOT	2ND PILOT	DUAL	1ST PILOT	2ND PILOT				
(2)	(3)	(4)	(5)	(6)	(7)	(8)	(9)	(10)	(11)	(12)	(13)	
292.05	2.50	2.10							4.40	14.40	4.10	

Malta's Part In Protecting Convoy

FIGHTERS DESTROY AT LEAST 13 RAIDERS

(Reuter's Service)

MALTA, August 16.

IT is now known that at least 13 Axis aircraft were shot down into the sea by R.A.F. fighters protecting the British convoy which safely reached Malta on Thursday. Many more Axis aircraft were damaged.

During the past few days so vital for Malta, R.A.F. fighters enjoyed absolute mastery of the skies over the Island. Reconnaissance aircraft kept a close watch on the progress of the convoy and when the ships entered "Bomb Alley," coming within fighter range of Malta, R.A.F. fighters took off, carrying out continuous patrols from first light to dusk. The Axis aircraft shot down were mostly bombers attempting to attack the convoy on its last lap.

The efforts of the British fighters, however, cannot be assessed merely on the numbers of enemy aircraft destroyed. Equally important was the deterrent effect they had on the Axis 'planes. Their 'planes dropped dozens of bombs harmlessly into the sea. The bombers who tried conclusions with the R.A.F. fighters were given a very bad time.

The protection of the convoy from the air was only made possible by the fact that the R.A.F. 'Spitfires' have achieved local air superiority.

"This morning the convoy was subjected to both dive-bombing and high-level attacks by both German and Italian aircraft, who themselves had strong fighter protection. During the combats which took place our "Spitfires" inflicted the following casualties on the enemy, according to details available at the time when this communique was issued:.

DESTROYED — One German bomber and two Italian bombers.

DAMAGED — Five German bombers of which one was so badly mauled that it had only the faintest hope of reaching home.

MALTA CONVOY

CONVOY STARTED OUT WITH 14 SHIPS & ESCORT. WITH 3 AIRCRAFT CARRIERS. [THE EAGLE WAS SUNK & FURIOUS DAMAGED] AFTER MANY FIERCE BATTLES WE MANAGED TO GET THREE MERCHANTMEN IN ON THURS. NIGHT. 13th. WITH TWO LAGGERS. ONE OF THE LAGGERS CAME IN ON AFTERNOON OF 14th. THE OTHER CAME IN LATER. MAKING FIVE IN ALL.

| 300.10 | 2.50 | 2.10 | | | | | | | 4.40 | 14.40 | 4.10 |

Logbook entry – Convoy.

British ports during the July of 1942, twelve large merchant ships were assembled and loaded with cargoes of ammunition, aircraft spares, food and medical supplies. Also on board was fuel, but carried in such small quantities that it was clear a tanker would be needed in the convoy. This came in the shape of the *Ohio*, a modern American ship built for the Texas Oil Company (now Texaco) in 1940. Another American vessel, the fourteenth ship, joined the fleet at the end of July. The convoy was to be escorted by aircraft carriers, battleships, cruisers and destroyers and was to be the largest as well as the most heavily escorted Allied convoy of the war sent to Malta. This was Operation Pedestal, a name that was to acquire a special place in the hearts of the beleaguered Maltese, in those of the British who took part in it and, indeed, in the British public back home.

As soon as the convoy was within range of the island, all three squadrons gave continuous cover to it. It had already been severely attacked and had lost quite a few ships by the time we reached it. On one of the sorties we had four Spitfires. We arrived just as it was being badly bombed by the Italians. As we came within range, I spotted a bomber doing a run in on one of the ships. It was a Breda 88 carrying a full bomb load. I managed to do a beam shot on it, allowing about eight rings deflection. My fire, from nose to tail, shot it out of the sky, and I flew through its debris. While this was happening the ships were pooping off everything they could find, and flak clouds from them were highly dangerous from our point of view. The convoy limped nearer to Malta, its losses severe. Fourteen ships plus escorts had started out, including the carriers *Eagle* and *Furious*. *Eagle* was sunk, and *Furious* too damaged to be able to continue with the convoy. We managed to cover three ships into Valletta harbour with two 'laggers' to get in by nightfall. The last to limp in on the fourteenth was the tanker *Ohio*, severely bombed and, incredibly, carrying the remains of a Stuka on the stern. The efforts to protect its precious cargo and to get it into port had been heroic. Frantic in their relief, the jubilant crowds came out to wave the *Ohio* into port, knowing only too well that had this convoy not got through Malta would have fallen and the course of the war dramatically changed.

After the August convoy came the October blitz. All had been quiet for a while with few air raids. The Axis powers now decided it was time to wipe us off the island. With this final push, they flung everything that could get airborne in their attack on Malta and we, in turn, flung ourselves back at them. The first wave saw about fifteen Ju88s in loose formation with an escort of twenty-five Macchi 202s and four 109s heading towards Malta. We were ready to face them and were scrambled for every raid, taking rest between raids from the searing Malta sun in the shade of our Spitfire wings, the quickest way to get airborne. Starting from when we were strapped in by crew and the engine started by battery trolley, we could be off the runway and airborne within five minutes. There were occasions when we were down to four serviceable aircraft and it was at these times that we used the four squadron tactics mentioned earlier, much safer in that we could keep an eye out for one another, there being no 'arse-end charlie' to lose. During October, I shot down most of my kills; on the twelfth, three down in one sortie, and on the thirteenth, two more.

The 12 October sortie had seen us scrambled to intercept a large formation of Ju88s which was being escorted by Me109s. The bombers were reported to be at 6,000 feet, so we climbed flat out to get above them at 15,000 feet. By now, all the other

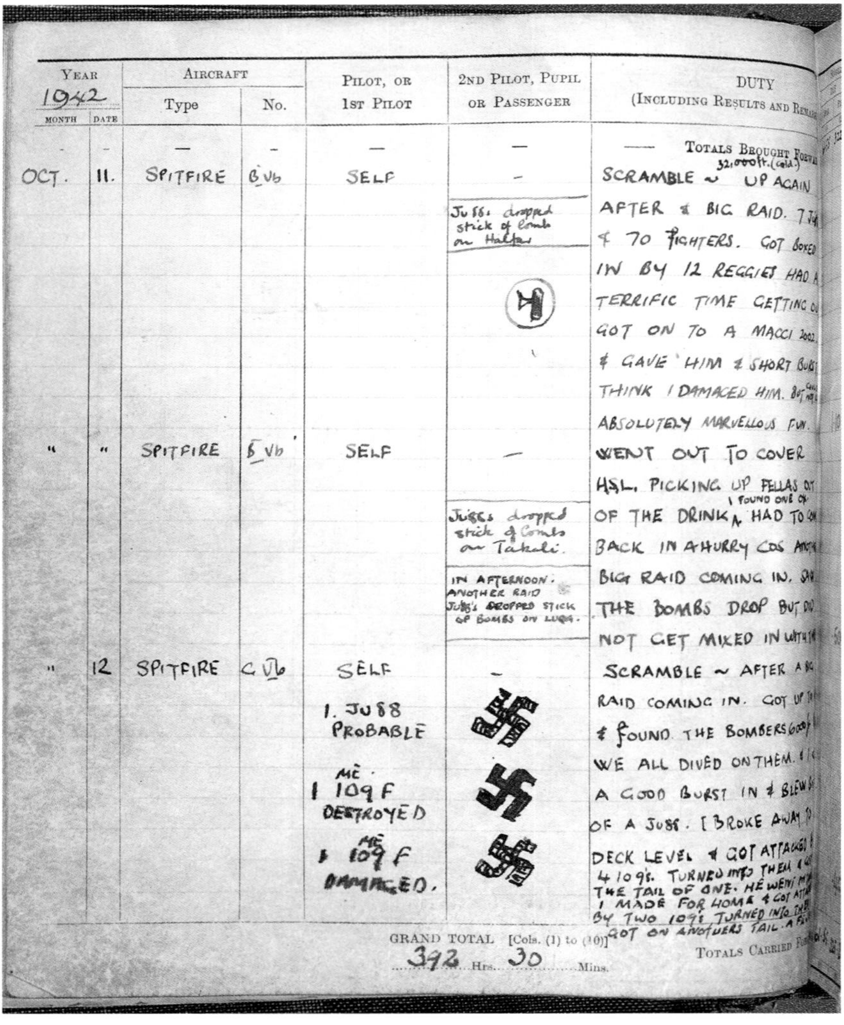

YEAR 1942 MONTH	DATE	AIRCRAFT Type	No.	PILOT, OR 1ST PILOT	2ND PILOT, PUPIL OR PASSENGER	DUTY (INCLUDING RESULTS AND REMARKS)
-	-	—	-	—	—	—— TOTALS BROUGHT FORWARD 32,000ft. (cold.)
OCT.	11.	SPITFIRE	B Vb	SELF	- Ju88s dropped stick of bombs on Halfar	SCRAMBLE ~ UP AGAIN AFTER A BIG RAID. 7 Ju[illegible] & 70 FIGHTERS. GOT BOXED IN BY 12 REGGIES HAD A TERRIFIC TIME GETTING OUT. GOT ON TO A MACCI 2002 & GAVE HIM A SHORT BURST THINK I DAMAGED HIM. BUT [illegible] ABSOLUTELY MARVELLOUS FUN.
"	"	SPITFIRE	B Vb	SELF	— Ju88s dropped stick of bombs on Takali. IN AFTERNOON. ANOTHER RAID Ju88s DROPPED STICK OF BOMBS ON LUQA.	WENT OUT TO COVER HSL. PICKING UP FELLAS OUT OF THE DRINK, I FOUND ONE [illegible] HAD TO COME BACK IN A HURRY COS ANOTHER BIG RAID COMING IN. SAW THE BOMBS DROP BUT DID NOT GET MIXED IN WITH THEM
"	12	SPITFIRE	C Vb	SELF 1. Ju88 PROBABLE 1 ME 109F DESTROYED 1 ME 109F DAMAGED.	-	SCRAMBLE ~ AFTER A BIG RAID COMING IN. GOT UP [illegible] & FOUND THE BOMBERS [illegible] WE ALL DIVED ON THEM. I [illegible] A GOOD BURST IN & BLEW [illegible] OF A Ju88. I BROKE AWAY TO DECK LEVEL & GOT ATTACKED BY 4 109s. TURNED INTO THEM & GOT THE TAIL OF ONE. HE WENT [illegible] I MADE FOR HOME & GOT ATTACKED BY TWO 109s TURNED INTO THEM GOT ON ANOTHERS TAIL. A F[illegible]
GRAND TOTAL [Cols. (1) to (10)] 392 Hrs. 30 Mins.						TOTALS CARRIED FORWARD

Taking rest from the Malta sun between raids.

squadrons had been scrambled as more than a hundred Ju88s had been reported. Seeing the bombers below we immediately dived down to engage. I got my sights on an 88 and opened fire with a good three-second burst. Bits flew off it and an engine was hit, smoke pouring out. I had to break hard then to avoid an Me109 on my tail. A dogfight was in progress with Spitfires and 109s weaving all over the sky. I managed to destroy a 109 and damage another. With the need for the attacking fighters to reserve enough fuel to get back to base, these dogfights did not last long, and it was not often three could be bagged in one sortie. It had been a very successful outcome.

November brought only isolated raids from Sicily with occasionally perhaps two bombers and a few 109s which were easily dealt with. More supplies came through. With hardly any scrambles now, we resorted to attacking them for a change. Carrying two 250-lb bombs under our wings, we would bomb and strafe suitable targets on Sicily. On one such trip, our target was Gela aerodrome where I dropped my two bombs on a gun emplacement, hitting and destroying the guns and blowing them sky high. The flak was considerable. I could see 109s scrambling. It was time to go home.

December was quiet enough to get another convoy of supplies to the island; four merchant ships and another American tanker arrived untouched. No longer in combat, the squadrons had sufficient fuel to use long-range tanks and give protection much earlier than could have been managed in August and had the satisfaction of safely escorting it into Grand Harbour. It was the last convoy into Malta. But by then I was already on my way home. The siege of Malta had finally been lifted, the frantic race for survival slowed. It had been the longest siege in British history, and we were to be denied the fruits of our labours. Here, at last, was food arriving in quantity and I, having finished my tour of ops, was posted back to the UK. We stopped at Gibraltar en route and for the first time in six months were able to *eat*. Unfortunately, even the simplest nourishment, such as bread with real butter, was too rich for me and my stomach rejected it. What irony!

Chapter 7

Malta and Dogfighting

I have often been asked to give talks on my flying experiences and, particularly, to describe a dogfight, but the swift intensity of it almost defies analysis and the picture becomes elusive. However, I will attempt a description.

The sky would be filled with aircraft, all of them twisting, turning and diving, my head jerking with them, eyes flitting from one flick of a movement to another. All actions became instinctive and so rapid, from brain to body to manoeuvring the aircraft, that it is hard to imagine them separately. Ultimately, the machine became an extension of the mind, one pilot-machine against an enemy pilot-machine, each trying to outwit the other, each determined not to be defeated. The manoeuvrability of an aircraft was vital, and it was here that the Spitfire had the advantage. It was up to the pilot to use it skilfully.

Called to scramble, the squadron would climb at full throttle to gain as much height as possible as quickly as possible, in order to be above the approaching bombers. We knew, and accepted, that the escorting 109s would always be above us. Nevertheless, on sighting the bombers we would individually pick our targets and dive to attack. At this point the Me109s would target the Spitfires. My tactic was to go for the bomber in a turn as I knew this would give the turret gunners difficulty in getting the correct deflection on me. It would also give me sighting of any 109 preparing to attack as he would have to turn inside me in order to get deflection. The firepower I had was eight machine guns and two cannons each firing twenty rounds per second which, in a three-second burst, would deliver 600 rounds, usually sufficient to destroy the bomber. I had to close in from between 250 to 300 yards to get my cone of fire on target and in those brief three seconds it all became one movement – fire and break left. It was in the break that I could pick out an Me109 attacking, at which point the dogfight would start.

The 109s used many tactics themselves and one of these was to 'bunt', that is, to apply negative G without stalling the engine. Unlike the Spitfire, the engine in the 109 had petrol injection. This would mean that if a 109 pilot spotted an enemy aircraft sitting on his tail, he would push the stick forward to bunt into a steep dive. In order to follow, we would have to half roll and pull into the dive. This was often best avoided as he might be heading towards Sicily and therefore taking us away from Malta. Another of their tactics was the head-on attack. This was the most dangerous of all. With the cannon firing directly ahead through the nose cone, he could open fire sooner than the Spitfire which had to be within 300 yards to be effective. With each aircraft flying at 400 mph (a closing speed of 800 mph) that was impossible. Whenever a 109 headed straight at me, I would instinctively side-slip to the left believing that a yawing target would be difficult to hit. These encounters happened in a flash and were far too close for comfort. Not only did the hair stand up on end, there was always the risk that a new pair of trousers would be needed on landing – as well as a cigarette or two.

Malta was an incredible experience. I had been through the most intense and dangerous of times and without even a scratch of paint off my aircraft. The memories were extraordinary and the relief unbelievable. Someone had been watching over me. I had survived.

Chapter 8

Back in the UK

Having flown back in the December of 1942, I was given a long leave to get a well-earned rest and I spent some time with my parents who were treated, naturally enough, to a long account of my experiences. Like so many families at that time, my mother and father had the constant, agonising worry of me serving in the RAF and my older brother, Ron, in the army.

It was not until January that I received my next posting. During this period I had a summons from the Lord Chamberlain to attend an awards ceremony at Buckingham Palace. I was a sergeant pilot whilst in Malta and apparently, because I had destroyed more than five enemy aircraft, I had become an 'ace'. I was duly summoned to receive the DFM (Distinguished Flying Medal) from King George VI. I mention this episode to highlight an incident that occurred during my brief visit to the palace.

In my early days as a fighter pilot, I was encouraged to have a cigarette to calm the nerves after combat, a dogfight for instance. So I took to smoking, and it was at the palace during the waiting period when the Lord Chamberlain was going through the 'dos and don'ts' to be strictly adhered to, that myself and another pilot thought it would be a good idea to slip out for a quick smoke. To slip out meant going through a large patio door behind a curtain. This we duly did only to meet the two princesses, Elizabeth and Margaret, walking towards us on the balcony. To cut a long story short, Princess Elizabeth, who must have been about sixteen at the time, very politely advised us to return to the reception room as it was not permitted to be out on the balcony. Embarrassed, I think I bowed my head, apologised and very quickly disappeared behind the curtain. I rather cherish the memory of being admonished by the Queen seventy years ago. Perhaps if I am lucky enough to get to a hundred and to be the oldest Spitfire fighter pilot still remaining from the Malta siege, I may get to meet her again – and will mention it!

After the frantic time in Malta my next posting was to a non-operational flying unit at RAF Grangemouth in Stirlingshire, Scotland. Here I was to test Spitfires that had been under major overhaul and needed to be test-flown to pass as fully serviceable before returning to the squadrons. At this stage I was not a fully trained test pilot but had sufficient experience and knowledge of the Spitfire to detect any faults. For example, if the aircraft could not maintain level flight due to a severe drop in the wing (known as left or right wing low), this might be easily corrected by the ground crew with aileron adjustment. On occasions, however, it could be extremely difficult to overcome the fault as the dropping of the wing was so severe that it took a lot of experience and special flying to get the aircraft safely landed again. This kind of flying suited me and initiated my desire to become a trained test pilot in the future. At that time there were no restrictions, such as controlled airspace and air traffic control, which meant that I could fly anywhere and at any height. The sky was so empty it gave me every opportunity to aerobat and take the aircraft to its limits. Grangemouth aerodrome was situated very close to the Firth of Forth and I would sometimes fly out to May Island and the Bass Rock at North Berwick which meant passing the Forth railway bridge. The thought would often occur to me that it would be possible to fly under the main centre span of the bridge. The thought soon turned to impulse and became irresistible. I did it and nearly came a cropper. In my excitement, I had forgotten to take into account the defence balloons with their steel cables near the bridge on the approach from the sea. Too late, I was already heading for the centre span. Fortunately, it turned out that the cables had been close-hauled to the ships and were not therefore too near the bridge. This gave me sufficient space to turn and climb steeply away. It made me sweat a bit! The adrenalin had been in full flow as the feeling of being back in combat had returned, but I knew I had been stupid and flown irresponsibly. It was a lesson learnt, never to be repeated. Meanwhile, my testing of the Spitfires continued, sometimes flying up to nine aircraft a day. This way I certainly got to know every aspect of the machine and came to regard it as the best fighter of all time.

During the tour at RAF Grangemouth I was commissioned and became a very proud pilot officer. As such, in my shining new uniform and DFM, I was given the task of going out to various villages around the area to talk to the local Scottish folk about my war experience. The hope was to entice them to part with their pots and pans for the war effort and, significantly, to help construct more Spitfires. It must have worked as the pots and pans rolled in.

It was also at Grangemouth that I met my first girlfriend and fell in love. She was a 'wee Scots lassie'. From the age of eighteen I had been flying on ops and never had the chance to meet

Joyce in WAAF uniform.

43

girls. Besides which, it seemed to me it might be foolhardy to get serious when our life expectancy was so short. Because of the lack of sleeping accommodation at the station we had been billeted out to local homes. I had been very lucky indeed to have landed with the most excellent Scottish hosts who accepted me into their family and looked after all my needs; very lucky too to have met their daughter Joyce. It was a relationship that lasted for many months. Joyce's father was a master baker who had a shop in Falkirk and a main bakery in Grangemouth. We used to visit here primarily to enjoy the luxury of eating some sweets! As sugar was rationed they were hard to come by, but as a baker her father was allowed more for the business and would spare a little to make these treats. But, after eight months, in September 1943 my third tour of ops sent me away from RAF Grangemouth, down to 122 Squadron at Gravesend in Kent. Joyce kept in touch.

Chapter 9

Third Tour of Ops

In an extraordinary coincidence similar to my starting with 124 Squadron, no sooner had I joined my new squadron than it was transferred, this time from Gravesend to RAF Weston Zoyland near Bridgwater on the Somerset Levels. As the aerodrome was very near the sea it was a suitable spot for air-firing practice on drogues. These were funnel-shaped devices similar to a windsock and towed, in this instance, by an aircraft specially fitted for the purpose, a Miles Martinet. This was an enjoyable sort of flying, a bit different from attacking a bomber which tended to fire back at you and it was very good preparation before returning to operational flying. We spent a carefree month at Weston Zoyland and it was here that I discovered the lethal effects of scrumpy compared to a pint of ale.

But operational flying at Gravesend soon resumed. From here we flew mostly on fighter sweeps into France hoping we would meet up with the Luftwaffe – and in due course we did. A squadron of 109s was based at Abbeville in northern France. Their noses had been painted bright yellow. In the early days over the Channel, seeing this glaring feature would make my pulse race a bit; they were a dangerous foe. An alternative to this was to go out on bombing runs on targets carrying two 250-lb bombs.

Occasionally we would give fighter escort cover for Beaufighters or Mitchells on bombing runs to the Frisian Islands. With the Spitfire, this meant only short-range cover and it proved inadequate when we started accompanying the heavy four-engine US bombers, the Flying Fortress and the Liberator, which might be returning, for example, from Berlin, Magdeburg or Brunswick. We could only escort them short distances into France or Holland and stay with them until they were safely over the English Channel. The American strategy was to fly the bombers in boxes to give maximum firepower from the combined gun turrets. On one occasion we picked up the first of the boxes of Forts returning from a Berlin raid over Eindhoven near the Zuider Zee. The state these aircraft were in was quite incredible. One, with smoke pouring from one or two engines, had a hole in the fuselage big enough to drive a car through. These aircraft had flown out on beam. This was a radio signal sent out from RAF Manston to help the Americans, flying on instruments, to get back from Germany and would take them directly over Eindhoven. The Germans soon realised this and put a flak emplacement directly under the beam, from which they concentrated a cone of fire upwards. It devastated the bombers. The pilots' courage was unsurpassed. To see a box of aircraft ahead of them, flying through this intense onslaught and then maintaining a steady flight to go through it themselves, was unbelievable. There was no deviation from the beam.

To overcome the short-range problem, the squadron soon changed from Spitfires to Mustangs. These had been fitted with the Merlin engine and long-range ranks which enabled them to fly for five hours, ideal for giving long-range cover to the American bombers. As it was such a long distance, the whole route was split into sections. If our squadron had the section which was actually over the target of Berlin, for instance, we would fly out to Berlin and join the bombers to give them air cover from German fighters until they were leaving. We would then start to fly back and the next squadron of Mustangs would take over the cover for that particular section and so on, to protect the complete route. A typical example was a trip we did in April 1944 escorting the Forts back from Magdeburg. We flew over the Zuider Zee, then round the top of the heavily defended Ruhr (nicknamed 'Happy Valley') and over Münster. This was where the concentrated flak came up. To avoid this we had to climb and alter course. Although a smaller target than the bombers we were more vulnerable. A piece of shrapnel piercing our single engine, or the 'glycol' (coolant), would mean the end of the machine and an inevitable bale-out, but it was usually the bombers flying beneath us that took the flak; our height meant we were comparatively free. We patrolled up and down as the Forts bombed their targets. Luckily, we had not so far encountered enemy fighters and I found myself having the time to look down at the devastation below. With the bombers moving out, the next squadron of Mustangs took over the next outward leg of the Forts. We were free then to set course for home with the hope that we would not get engaged with any Me109s. Fortunately on this occasion, we did not. I found that flying these long trips at 30,000 feet for four hours or so in a cramped, cold and unpressurised cockpit was daunting and tiring and certainly not as pleasant as flying the Spitfires. But at last we were able to give the fighter cover that had been so desperately needed.

As we were flying more often over enemy territory, there was concern that for pilots who had to bale out survival on the ground would be paramount. It was decided that practice at this would be a great asset. So the intelligence officers arranged a special exercise. Taking part, I joined up with a

Mustang.

fellow pilot with whom I had often flown as a pair. His name was Johnnie Meyer. We were transported to an unknown destination. Dressed as though we had baled out, in blue pullovers, scarf and flying boots, we were dumped out of the truck and told to find our way back to the station at Gravesend. All road signs and names on railway stations had, of course, been taken down early on in the war and the British countryside looked bleak. We could have been anywhere in Europe. The exercise was realistic.

We found ourselves in the middle of a field without a clue where we should go next. Our best plan of action, we concluded, would be to walk along the edge of the field in the hope of reaching a road. I had a button compass with me so that, on finding the road, we decided to head north. We duly edged our way slowly along. Suddenly out of nowhere, men with rifles at the ready appeared. Someone, most likely a farmer, must have spotted us and immediately called the Home Guard. Our exercise had not lasted long and it was all I could do to suppress a grin. We continued the role as we had been ordered to, that is, we had been forbidden to speak English. So after much gesturing, we put our hands up and walked ahead with the guards behind us, their rifles pointing at our backs. It was at this point that I began to feel rather nervous. From what they were saying, it was obvious they were convinced we were Germans and would certainly have shot us if we had tried any tricks. Johnnie, on the other hand, was thoroughly enjoying himself and entered into the spirit of the exercise fully, playing the convincing role of Luftwaffe crew who had baled out. John's father was Belgian and he could certainly play the part of a German very well, too well in fact, which made me all the more nervous. The young men gave all the signs of being trigger-happy and my companion's professional act was getting risky.

We arrived at last at a police station and were locked in a cell. It was not long before an army intelligence officer entered to interrogate us. He spoke slowly in pigeon English. Johnnie kept up his part and gave the officer a rough time, picking up a daily newspaper which happened to be in the cell, looking at it and throwing it down in disgust, shouting 'Propaganda!'.

I was most uncomfortable. The officer bristled and went red, picked up the paper and departed. Alone again, I told Johnnie that I thought it had gone far enough and that we should tell him we were on an RAF exercise and produce our ID cards, the 1250s. These were hidden in our flying boots. Johnnie agreed, eventually. What followed was even more uncomfortable. The surprise and anger on the face of the intelligence officer was apparent. He was not at all pleased and took a very dim view. Although the RAF had informed local areas of the dropping zones they were using, nobody had apparently told the little town, Green Street Green. There were apologies all round and we were eventually released. The exercise had shown us all too well how easily things could go wrong and in Europe, of course, the risk of getting shot was only too real. If you were lucky enough to stay alive, the alternative was not good either; many ended up 'in the bag'.

After the escapade of trying to be Germans, we got back to normal squadron life. By now it was mid 1944 and there seemed to be fewer daylight raids by the 'Forts and Libs', so we resorted to a different role. In April this took the form of escorting Beaufighters fitted with torpedoes that were on their way to attack a German convoy in the Frisian Islands. Our task was to give them fighter cover over the target. The flak was fierce, not only from the ships but from guns based on the islands mostly aimed at the attacking Beaus but bursts would get through to us circling above. I did witness one of the Beaufighters taking a direct hit. It must have caught the torpedo because there was an almighty flash before it went into the sea. However, the raid was successful as the convoy was completely destroyed. We escorted the remaining bombers back to base at a more reasonable height, a sharp contrast to the way we had gone out to the target. There is nothing more exhilarating than robbing the enemy of advanced warning by skimming over the waves at zero feet under radar cover.

A few more trips escorting the Forts followed in May but mostly we were now tasked with dive-bombing targets in France in preparation for the build-up to the D-Day invasion which we knew must be imminent but, of course, had no idea when. These attacks, carrying two 250-lb bombs attached under the wings of the Mustang, ran almost constantly each day into June. In one instance our target was an aerodrome near Lille where we pounded the hangars and then, with bombs gone, strafed parked aircraft with cannon fire. There was a small amount of flak but nothing to worry about. The following day, the target was the marshalling yards at St Quentin. I dropped my bombs on the engine sheds and then strafed trucks on a siding. This time there was no flak at all, which gave us the opportunity to concentrate on the targets without weaving. This kind of flying was now almost routine. How different our role had become. Previously it had all been about engaging enemy aircraft and getting into dogfights. Now we were looking for trouble without much success. But it was not all smooth running and we did have a few losses. In fact, we lost two COs with flak. They baled out.

Still, now and again an escort operation for the Forts and Libs would come up, especially on a target where they needed fighter cover. On one occasion this was Brunswick. Unfortunately, when we reached the position where we would pick them up, levels of cloud were obscuring the whole area and we were unable to find them. The CO decided that we should split into pairs, climb through the cloud and report the height of any layers of clearance that the Forts would be flying in and the squadron could climb to, and re-formate. Not being good at instrument-flying, I close formated with Johnnie and we entered cloud around 5,000ft. I had one hell of a time staying with him, not breaking cloud until 34,000ft. I sweated all the way up that ascent until I was hugely relieved to see the sun at last. Of course, at this height the Forts would certainly not be flying, which meant that now we had to make the nerve-racking descent. I can't describe the task I had given myself to close formate on another aircraft in thick cloud. It was as terrifying as dogfighting with an Me109 on the tail, catching the wink of his cannon fire before screwing the tightest turn imaginable to escape. Through it all came the incessant cold, salty sweat running down the face and into the mouth. We broke cloud over the Zuider Zee and I was so relieved to see the deck again I almost choked. We were greeted with flak, which seemed like a cruel welcome after what we had been through. Johnnie said he had been hit and would have to bale out. I flew around him but could see no damage. I managed to calm him down and, as we were so close to the sea, to persuade him to head back to Manston. But we were not out of trouble yet. There was always that anxious alertness for any 109s. Had they been around, we would have ended up in a dogfight, which did not appeal to me at the time, but we managed to creep out and belt back to the good old white cliffs as fast as we could. This was an experience I never wanted to repeat but, believe me, it was the most effective lesson. It made me determined to become more proficient at instrument-flying. During my initial training, I had been graded 'below average' for instrument-flying but 'above average' for flying. Later on, with much practice flying twins and four-engine aircraft, I found I could cope well with the instruments.

D-Day came and the skies were clear and quiet. That was it for me. I had finished my third tour of ops and had leave before my next posting for non-operational flying.

Chapter 10

Testing

After a short course at Bedford I was ready. The next posting was to be as a test pilot. This was great! Not only was I being posted to Maintenance Units (MUs) around the country but I was also attached to civilian firms such as Vickers-Armstrong at High Post, Salisbury where all aircraft to be tested came direct from the factory. Here I had the good fortune to meet and fly with Jeffrey Quill and Mike Lithgow, two very experienced test pilots. I learnt quickly from them and built up valuable experience for the future. I remember Jeffrey, the chief test pilot, always wearing white overalls, while the distinctive memory I have of Mike is when he tried to put an aero engine into an ordinary car. We set off towards Salisbury in this supercharged vehicle, but the engine was too powerful and nearly took the car apart. Both men let me get on with my flying undisturbed but were very good at giving guidance when needed, especially when it was my turn to climb into brand-new factory aircraft. Many years later I met Jeffrey again. It was at Hendon at the launch of *Aces High*. We pilots, aces all, sat at a long table and signed against our names.

Test flying from the MUs was vital in order to get the aircraft up to military standards and to ensure that they were safe before being despatched to the squadrons. It was marvellous to be posted to these units because each had several different types of aircraft to test. I was issued with the blue-covered, metal-ringed Ferry Notes, full of vital information for flying many different aircraft types. It was while testing these that I experienced several 'near squeaks' and the occasional crash. The most interesting, and perhaps the most dangerous of these, are detailed later.

After leaving 122 Squadron my first posting was to 39 MU Colerne on 27 June 1944, a Fighter and Bomber Command aerodrome on the outskirts of Colerne village in Wiltshire. Here I flew mainly Spitfires and Seafires with other types such as Anson, Oxford, Master and Blenheim thrown in for good measure. It was at Colerne the following year that I had my first near squeak as a test pilot flying a Master (described later). That did nothing to lessen fond memories of the station. It was an extremely friendly, welcoming place, not just in the test crew room but in other sections too. WAAF Flight Officer Desirée Hair's bubbly and vivacious personality rubbed off on to anyone talking to her, including me. She was based in the equipment section, had golden-coloured hair and wore an Australian emblem on the upper sleeve of her uniform. We soon became good friends and spent many happy times together. Addicted to speed, most pilots have to travel as fast as possible on land as well as in the air and so, true to form, I had bought

Dessie and myself at RAF Colerne.

a motorcycle, not just any old model but an Ariel Square Four 1000 cc, an extremely fast machine for its day. It was not long before Dessie was joining me riding pillion. We would go on trips round the Cotswolds, Dessie clutching me tightly round my waist, a nice, comforting feeling, while I accelerated up to eighty plus on the straights. The roads were almost empty of traffic, there were no speed limits to spoil the fun and no helmets. With hair blowing in the wind, my Irvin jacket keeping me warm and Dessie relishing the speed behind me, we shared some great times. My next posting to Kemble, however, brought it to an end but in that summer of 1944, wondering perhaps what the war and the world had to offer us in the future, we parted good friends. The future was to prove 1944 would not quite be the end of the story.

Finding myself now in Gloucestershire and the Cotswolds, 5 MU Kemble gave me the opportunity to fly Typhoons and Tempests as the main output, with Lysanders and others as secondary. In July 1944 I attended the morning briefing in the crew room and was asked to pick up a Lysander which had been stored for some time in one of the satellite fields, Blakehill (or possibly Slade) Farm. It appeared this aircraft had been kept there and used for dropping and picking up secret agents to and from France. It was obvious it had been in that field a considerable time and it would be a matter of luck if we could get it started. Having arranged transport and a crew of 'fitter and rigger', we were ready to go when a young Flying Officer approached me. He told me he was from Signals and was particularly interested in the signal set-up in the rear cockpit. Could he join me on the flight? I had to point out to him the dangers of flying an old aircraft that had been stored in a field for God knew how long, in addition to the implications of trying to fly it out from that very same small field. Anything, I warned him, could happen, which is why they had asked a test pilot, and not a ferry pilot, to do it. He seemed undaunted and flattered me by referring to my record as a pilot. I told him flattery would get him nowhere. We climbed into the waiting transport.

Blakehill/Slade Farm was only a few miles away so we soon found ourselves there. We clambered out of the truck and into a grass field roughly the size of two football pitches and surrounded by hedges. Looking around me, my first impression was that this was a bit dicey for take-off but the crew had wasted no time in getting to work. They had found the 'Lizzy' in a barn at the end of the field and soon got cracking on her. The engine was running in no time.

Young Jakes was looking dubiously at the Lizzy, so I tried to reassure him. It was an ugly thing, huge with its high wing towering above us, large wheel spats and a ladder down the side of the fuselage from the back of the cockpit which I told him was for the agents to get out quickly when dropped. But it did the job for short take-offs, vital for those missions into France. We managed to push it out of the barn and clambered up to the cockpit. I sat in and did my checks, making absolutely sure that I had set the tail trim to neutral. This was important as the whole of the tailplane would alter, unlike normal trims with a tab. If it was left in a backward position it would almost loop the loop on a take-off run. I signalled to the crew to remove the chocks and we were ready to go. I shouted to Jakes that we were ready for the off and would be out of the field in no time. With fifteen degrees of flap and the large leading edge slots open, we rushed towards the hedge. I am not sure my back passenger felt the same confidence.

But we made it. Once airborne, I climbed away, turned left towards the Fosse Way, which was easy to pick out, and caught sight of Kemble. But I thought I wouldn't go in just yet. I wanted to have a fly around and give the young Signals lad a trip he could work out from the rear cockpit. It was not to be. I started to have a little trouble maintaining the height and then a voice from the rear piped up to inform me that I must have flown through a flock of birds as they had shot past his window. I told him that we hadn't hit any birds but that he should check his harness as we might have to do a forced landing. There was silence from the back. As it was so near, I decided to head for Kemble and try to make the perimeter or the end of the runway. I warned air traffic and asked to

Lysander (drawing courtesy Martin Bourne).

have a clear runway. The Lysander was stable enough to keep steady but was descending rapidly like an elevator. Kemble, thankfully, was approaching. I managed to make the end of the runway and gave almost full throttle to try and flare out, but it hit the ground heavily. At least those huge wheel spats didn't come up to meet me. Having given so much throttle we charged down the runway and, coming to an eventual stop, we clambered out. The sight that met our eyes was quite something. The fabric had completely peeled off the wing, making it look like a skeleton. Thankfully, the large metal leading edge and the slots were intact, and it was this marvellous construction that had given me sufficient lift to remain airborne, albeit briefly. Thank God, I thought, that the tailplane remained intact. Jakes was a bit shaken. The birds that he thought he had seen were, of course, the strips of fabric from the wing. I think I managed to persuade him to stick to normal flights in the future. We had been lucky that time; we had both survived.

While flying at Kemble I was sent to White Waltham on a refresher course to get reacquainted with heavy twins. Up to then, I had only been flying light twin aircraft such as the Anson and Oxford. White Waltham was a civil ATA unit and I believe I was the only RAF officer on the course so I found myself flying with civil airline captains. This proved to be quite interesting as their way of flying was so different from the RAF's. Here I was to fly a Hudson and an Albermarle. The instructor was to be Captain Warne, a civil captain, teamed with two civil pilots, Captains Geoff Greenhalge and Bill Bailey. Geoff had been flying a DH89 Dragon Rapide from Speke Liverpool Airport to the Isle of Man, and Bill, from Renfrew, Glasgow, had been shuttling to and from the Isles. They were both converting to the heavier twin as the airline company British European Airways (BEA) was soon to add Vikings to its fleet. It was not long before I was flying as first pilot and finished the short course, passing to fly heavy twins. I duly returned to my unit. During this time, I got to know these two pilots well and they tried to convince me that if ever I should leave the RAF they would give me their full support.

It was around this time that I heard the awful news of my brother's death. Ron had been a despatch rider with the Royal Artillery and, following the D-Day invasion, was caught by a sniper's bullet near Goch in North Rhine-Westphalia, Germany. He was twenty-nine and left a widow and two children in Liverpool. He is buried in the Reichswald Forest War Cemetery near the Dutch border. My father was to die shortly afterwards, leaving my mother alone now except for myself – and I had not chosen the safest of jobs.

By December 1944, with demand from the squadrons lessening, the testing programme had reduced considerably. As a result, when the ferry pool at Aston Down in Gloucestershire asked for some help, I was very happy to be detailed. It would give me several more types of aircraft to fly. It was while flying a Tiger Moth from Hooton Park in Cheshire to Aston Down that I had a most strange experience.

The weather had been clear with good visibility until I reached the Malvern Hills. From then on the ground was completely covered by fog. I continued on track and timing, hoping that this fog was only local and that Aston Down would be clear. This was not to be. At the time I should have been there, I could see nothing. There was no radio transmission in the

Tiger Moth so I could not call up air traffic control. I was stuck. I was just considering returning north when, amazingly, the fog cleared just enough to make a hole and show the ground beneath, not any old piece of ground but an aerodrome with a runway, all clearly visible. Instinctively, I did a vertical side slip through the gap then levelled out over the runway and landed. By the time I had taxied along to find the perimeter, the fog had closed in again but with sufficient forward visibility for me to continue taxiing. Air traffic control, and it was Aston Down, were astonished to see a Tiger Moth emerging from the fog and heading towards them. I felt the same sense of grateful relief that was, by now, beginning to grow familiar and to reinforce the sense that I truly *was* born to survive. Several interesting test flights followed and each of these was to strengthen this belief:

39 MU Colerne, Cotswolds 18 July 1945
Miles Master: starboard wing folded back from root on approach just over the lights. Instinctively stuffed everything, stick and rudder, to the right-hand corner of the cockpit. Crash-landed to the right of the threshold. Broke up a bit but managed to climb out unhurt.

19 MU St Athan, South Wales 10 November 1945
Buckmaster: really bad weather, very poor visibility. Had to land with undercarriage red lights and horn blowing. A dicey moment not knowing if undercarriage would collapse. Landed OK.

St Athan 28 February 1946
Beaufighter: tyre burst on landing.

St Athan 23 July 1946
Mosquito: on take-off. Large dip three-quarters down on runway. Air traffic failed to clear runway of seabirds roosting in the dip. Flew through them at full throttle, fracturing main spar, starboard wing. Warned air traffic, completed a careful circuit. Landed successfully.

27 MU Shawbury, Shropshire 3 October 1946
Mosquito: port engine CSU (constant speed unit) failed on

take-off when just airborne. Aircraft swung violently to left heading towards corner of MU Hangar situated on end. Fail to understand how I got round but managed it and landed eventually, with difficulty. Corner of hangar now bears plaque named 'Scott's Corner' (Green Endorsement – the RAF accolade for safely landing in difficult circumstances).

Shawbury 16 January 1947
Wellington: port engine cut on take-off. Controlled with no difficulty.

Shawbury 18 March 1947
Mosquito: similar to flights with Beaufighters at St Athan. Radar operator in side seat testing radar equipment guided me to target (his first time). I entered cloud, fortunately broke cloud before entering rear gun turret of a Halifax. Broke violently to miss it. Did not fly with that operator again.

A particular incident at Shawbury is etched on my memory. It happened on 20 March 1947. Flt Lt Stan Hedley was under training to be an MU test pilot and had been detached to 27 MU Shawbury for familiarisation and experience on the twin-engine Mosquito before returning to the MU at Driffield to test them. On that day I decided to take Flt Lt Hedley on a test flight to give him experience flying on only one of its engines. The weather was fair with good visibility and a cloud base of at least 10,000 feet, ideal for this test.

   We took off from Shawbury and climbed to 5,000 feet. I feathered the starboard engine, flew and showed the capabilities of the Mosquito on one engine. In fact, I did a roll to demonstrate how good it was. Having then unfeathered the starboard engine and put it back to normal, I feathered the port engine and followed the same procedure without any problem. But this was where our troubles began. In spite of several goes, I could not get the port engine unfeathered. There was nothing for it. We would have to do a one-engine landing for real and I told Stan as much. This was not what he had been expecting, of course. As we approached Shawbury I explained to him that there was usually no problem in landing providing the pilot kept above 180 knots until on final approach when committed to landing.

Below this speed, the rudder would start to kick violently and control of it would be lost. Having explained all this carefully to Stan, I started my approach to Shawbury, contacting air traffic control for a priority landing, which was given. I continued to turn on to final approach, undercarriage down, fifteen degrees of flap, speed at 185 knots. All was well. As I approached, I had observed that a York was taxiing towards the runway threshold. Usual procedure would be for the York to hold, do his checks and allow the approaching aircraft to land and so I continued to concentrate on my landing. To my horror, the York taxied on to the threshold of the runway and prepared to take off. My expletive was more than 'crikey'. There was only one thing for it. I would have to overshoot and go round again, *the* most dangerous procedure of all to carry out successfully on a Mosquito. If I opened the throttle more than a trickle, it would flick violently towards the dead engine and crash into the ground.

By now, with the speed below 180 knots, the rudder pedals were kicking madly, left to right, right to left. I selected the undercarriage 'up' and as there was only one pump working from the good engine, I told Stan that if we wanted to live, he would have to help it with the 'wobble pump' which was on the side of my seat. He knelt down facing me and, clutching the handle of the pump, started to waggle it frantically. I have never in my life seen a pump handle move so fast, it almost disappeared in a blur. Clearly, the adrenalin was doing its own frantic pumping through his veins.

By this time the Mosquito had drifted to one side of the runway and we were flying crab-wise parallel to the York taking off. I was inching open the throttle extremely carefully, bit by bit, to give me more power and to hold level flight. Stan had managed to get the undercarriage up and clean. We were holding level flight. I thanked God we had cleared that hurdle; we could so easily have ploughed into the deck. Cold sweat was by now pouring off me. The last time that had happened was in combat when an Me109 was sitting on my tail. The York, now climbing away, was leaving us rocking in his slipstream. Holding at 500 feet, I continued to take up the flaps very slowly until I was clean and could fly normally on one engine. Once clean I started to climb to 1,000 feet and then to fly around the well-known and much-loved Shropshire landmark, the Wrekin (1335 ft/ 407m high).

But we could at least relax for a while and start to think about contacting air traffic. They had been frantically trying to contact me while the crash crew, equally frantically, had been trying to follow me. But on seeing that I was maintaining height and climbing, they returned to base. Air traffic explained that the York had had no radio transmission contact and that they had been helpless to stop it. I entered the circuit, apologised for not being able to contact them, explaining that I had been 'rather busy' and asked them to please give me a priority landing for a one-engine landing.

We landed safely. Back in the crew room I told Stan that that had been the most dangerous flying I had ever done in my

With a Mosquito – on a calmer occasion.

life and that we had been lucky to get away with it. I added that I hoped he would never have to go through an experience like that again when he started to fly the Mosquito. Unfortunately, this was not to be. In an amazing coincidence, Stan Hedley did have to carry out a one-engine overshoot and was killed in doing so.

I had survived this incident, as many others. When I came to think about it, I realised that the twentieth of March was my father's birthday. I believe he had been my guardian angel in this as he had throughout those long, hard combat days.

Throughout all this time, Joyce had kept in touch by letter, but it was during my posting to 27 MU Shawbury that I met my future wife Pat. Writing to Joyce to tell her we must part was extremely distressing. I felt very guilty because I knew how she would be feeling on reading it.

Pat, the prettiest girl I had ever seen, who became my wife.

Pat Harper was the welfare officer for the MU and the prettiest girl I had ever seen. It seemed the only way I could get acquainted with her was to go to an MU dance, not a hopeful opportunity as I was a very poor ballroom dancer. A Scottish reel or the Dashing White Sergeant I could have managed skilfully enough, but it was highly unlikely that I would be given the opportunity to shine with those! Determined not to be thwarted, I asked her for a dance anyway. She turned out to be an extremely good dancer and managed to steer me successfully, which broke the ice with us both laughing. From then on, we met regularly, going out for runs in the car whenever possible. I suppose she must have been taken with a dashing test pilot, because when I eventually asked her to marry me she accepted. The wedding was at St Cuthbert's Church in Carlisle where her mother was living at the time, her father having recently died. Rationing made it difficult to get a full wedding dress but somehow this was managed. I was in uniform as was my best man, a fellow RAF officer and a very old friend, David Prestwich. Rationing hit not only the efforts to acquire the dress but also in limiting the reception (we were allowed a maximum of twenty-five guests) and shortening our journey for the honeymoon. I had enough petrol to get us to Ayr and to a suite in the main hotel. It was 5 June 1948.

Chapter 11

Crossroads

At the end of December 1947 I remembered my short course at White Waltham and the two civil pilots from BEA with whom I had become friendly. It seemed to me at that point in my RAF life that a move to BEA would be a good idea as it was nearing the time when I would have to make a decision as to whether or not I wanted to stay in for a further commission. I decided to relinquish my RAF identity card (the 1250), but it was with a heavy heart that I let it go. It felt too much like giving up my right arm.

My first task was to obtain a civilian pilot's licence. This meant joining a two-week civilian course in London. Finding somewhere to stay in the capital was a problem, and the only digs I could track down were in Greenwich. This meant a lot of daily travelling, which I was to find extremely difficult. When I had joined the RAF in 1940, traffic had been much lighter, and I had no experience of a crowded thoroughfare. This was foreign territory to me.

The first mode of transport I started to use was the Underground. Standing on the platform waiting for the train to arrive, the whole place seemed to become one heaving mass of people that would carry me along with it towards the next arrival, whether I wanted that train or not. Once inside, the doors would close on the mass of humanity, with me wedged somewhere inside it. When the train stopped at the next station the doors would open and once again, to my horror, I would be literally walked out on to the platform. This form of transport was not for me! I started to investigate the alternatives. I was told that the overland trains from Greenwich might be the answer.

As I stood on Greenwich station platform waiting for the train to arrive, it seemed to me the crowd of people was not that far off what I had seen on the Underground. The train pulled in and, again, a mighty rush of bodies made for the doors and into the carriage, filling up not only the seats but the standing positions in the middle. To my mind we were already crowded to the limit but not according to the porter, who proceeded to push more in almost to the point where the far end passenger was halfway out of the window.

To my amazement one morning, I saw a man sitting down and almost on his lap was another man's bottom. The seated man calmly put his newspaper, already prepared into a folded square, in front of him under the bottom and started to read. I could not believe what I was seeing and nearly fell into hysterical laughter. I noticed the same man the next day, and many days afterwards and began to watch him with interest. He would arrive at the station, walk to a selected spot by a drainpipe, prop himself against it and start to fold his paper into a square. When the train arrived, he would walk forward like a robot to a carriage door directly in front of him. Each day he repeated exactly the same procedure. I could not get used to this kind of life!

There was just one more mode of transport left for me to try – the good old red London bus. But even this was not without its quirks. On one occasion I had walked to Westminster Bridge to give myself a little exercise. Here I boarded the Plumstead bus and managed to get a seat, one of those that face each other near the door. At the next stop an old lady boarded and stood in front of me, so I immediately stood up and offered her my seat. She sat down. Meanwhile, the conductor, who had been on the upper deck, came down and stood on the platform looking into the lower deck. He started to count from one to five. When he reached six, he shouted 'Five only downstairs!' and, looking at me, told me I would have to get off. I protested and tried to explain but was firmly put off. The old girl to whom I had given my seat was, amazingly, struck dumb. She just sat there without batting an eyelid. I was speechless. To hell with London, I thought, and was only too glad to get out of the place when my course finished!

The next step after completing the training was to get in touch with one of the BEA captains I had met at Kemble and start the ball rolling towards civilian flying. I joined the company, but my employment was to be very short, in fact a mere six months. At the end of that time I was made redundant. It was all too sudden. I was stunned to find myself so quickly out of a job. My first thought was how I could get back into the RAF where I had felt safe and happy. Undaunted I got in touch with a good friend, a Group Captain who was working in the Air Ministry, and asked him if there was any chance. It would not be easy, he warned, but assured me he would try every avenue to get me reinstated. I was accepted in the end, primarily I think because I was a test pilot. However, there was a sting in the tail. I would have to lose twelve years' seniority and there would be no prospect of promotion. I was only too glad to accept; I was back in the family, so to speak. To my astonishment I found myself at 27 MU Shawbury again, once more in a military pilot's seat and testing Vampires and Mosquitoes as though I had never left.

But my return to the fold was not without its consequences. On December 8, 1948, at Shawbury, I had my final crash whilst testing. I had made a rule when first test-flying that a crash through aircraft error would be an acceptable part of the job. But if it was through pilot error then it would be time to call it a day, and I would quit testing.

On this day I made an error which proved contributory to the aircraft crashing. Strangely, it was a procedure I had carried out many, many times but on this occasion my memory was at fault. I had feathered the engine and, on unfeathering, had failed to check that the button had not released. I would normally have put my fingers behind the button and pulled it out. Strangely again, it was in a Mosquito, an aircraft with which I seem to have had a peculiar fascination in finding fault. I crashed with a runaway port engine (revs 6000 rpm

Low flying during aerobatic display.

After a successful display at one of the airshows.

plus), hitting the ground at a speed of 180 knots. The aircraft
broke up completely, but the cockpit remained intact. When
it came to a halt I climbed out unscathed, once again surviv-
ing to walk away. But my own rule had been broken, and I had
to face the prospect of giving up testing. It was not until May
1950 that I actually stopped, however.

By 1952 I found that I was being asked to do several air displays.
For these I flew mostly Vampires as it seemed to be the most
successful aircraft for such events; it was fast and the whistling
sound of the jet engine when it passed over the spectators' heads
at a low height (these were the days before the crowd line rule)
gave them the thrilling indication of tremendous speed. I would
use 'Scott's Corner' in particular to accentuate this manoeuvre.

Chapter 12

Final Crash, 1953

Having finally finished testing, I retired to fly light aircraft and relax but my reputation for giving air displays must have followed me as again and again I was asked to display at various functions. For these I usually flew Tiger Moths. They were ideal for aerobatics at low altitude and quite safe, providing I kept well clear of the spectators. Stationed at RAF Turnhouse, Edinburgh, I was given a driver, Alan Livingstone, to motor me around the aerodrome. While at Turnhouse I was asked to do an air display for the pupils of Fettes College. I agreed readily and used the station Tiger Moth for it.

It was a fine day in October, warm enough for the boys to stand out on the aerodrome. I stayed at 500 feet for this display except when more height was needed for aerobatics such as loop the loop or when carrying out my favourite manoeuvre, the vertical side slip from 1000 feet to the ground to land. I did actually carry out this manoeuvre but didn't land. I opened the throttle, climbed back to 500 feet but then felt that something was wrong. The Tiger started to dive towards the ground. Immediately, I tried to pull the stick back but found that it was jammed. Fortunately, I was heading away from the boys towards the Turnhouse golf course which was just over the road by the aerodrome boundary. At 500 feet, I could not bale out. I had to accept the inevitable – I was going to crash into the ground ahead. As I was plummeting towards it, I remembered that I had switched the engine off. It flashed through my mind that at least there should not be a fire on impact.

I remember nothing more of the crash. The rest of the narrative must be taken up with information given to me by my wife and other witnesses.

It seemed that the reason I had been unable to move the control column back into my stomach was because the stern post had broken and jammed the elevators in the down position (clearly shown in the picture on p 71). This particular Tiger Moth was of wooden construction. Apparently it was woodworm in the stern post that had caused the weakness and with the side pressure applied to it during the display it snapped. The crash crews and RAF ambulance rushed to the scene which was the practice ground for the golf course. At the time a golf professional was giving a lesson when I crashed in front of him. It was he who ran over and dragged me clear.

Having examined the crash, the investigating team issued their report. On impact with the ground I had been ejected from the rear cockpit, which catapulted me over the petrol tank situated on the upper wing directly in front of the cockpit. In the process, I had caught my face and my right arm and right leg on the tank, damaging them severely. I then continued on to land on the ground a few feet in front of the aircraft. It was then that Mr Turnbull, the golf professional, had come running over to drag me clear, although this was unnecessary as I was well away from the aircraft and it had not caught fire. I was picked up by the ambulance and rushed into Edinburgh Royal Infirmary. My wife by this time had grown used to visits by an OC Flying or an orderly officer (an officer on general duties) to inform her of my latest escapade – there had been so many of them – and would have my 'small kit' packed and ready. Now, seeing an RAF car pulling up outside our home and a tall Squadron Leader stepping out, Pat opened the door with the words 'Which hospital is he in now?', stopping the officer in his tracks, his mouth dropping in surprise. Arriving at the hospital, she was met this time by the consultant who told her of the seriousness of the accident. Her first sight of me confirmed what she had just heard. She recalled later that I looked a dreadful mess, that I had no face and that face and shoulders were all one (whatever that meant). Nevertheless, as awful as

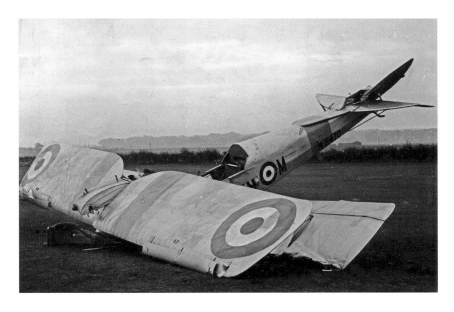

The final crash – Tiger Moth, October 1953.

I must have looked, Pat accepted what she had seen and remained her usual calm self, which impressed the consultant accompanying her.

There followed a slow process of recovery. I was kept at the infirmary until the swelling had reduced to the point where I had some shape of a face and was then transferred to the plastic surgery hospital at Bangour near Livingston adjacent to the masts at Kirk o'Shots. There followed many operations performed by several different consultants: Mr Wallace who built my face; Mr Kerr, an Australian, my nose, and Mr McKlennan, a Scottish surgeon, my mouth. Throughout my stay up to now, I was blind and I remember the eye surgeon arriving at my bedside each day and informing me that he was shining a light in my eyes. If I could see the light I was to wave my left hand (my only moveable part). Each day I strived to see that light. The nurse who attended me in the special care unit was a constant companion and because I was not able to see her, nor could I ask my wife what she looked like (I could not talk for six months), I let my imagination run riot. She had a Scandinavian accent, so I visualised her as the most lovely blonde with vivid blue eyes. One day the eye surgeon came to do his usual visit of shining the light into my eyes, but this time it was different – I could see it, the most beautiful sight I could ever have imagined. If I had had a mouth I would have whooped for joy but I could only waggle my left hand frantically. There was great excitement all round.

From then on my recovery went from strength to strength and I knew I was going to be all right. With my blindfolds removed I was able to see again the wonderful wife who had come in almost daily from Edinburgh to visit. Alan Livingstone, my driver, had been extremely kind throughout this time, driving her to Bangour Hospital whenever he was not on duty. I was also able to confirm the vision of my Scandinavian nurse; she really was everything I had imagined – a blonde and blue-eyed stunner!

Soon I was walking round the ward and impatient to get well. As one of the consultants lived in Edinburgh, he agreed for me to go home and for Pat to care for me. He would visit

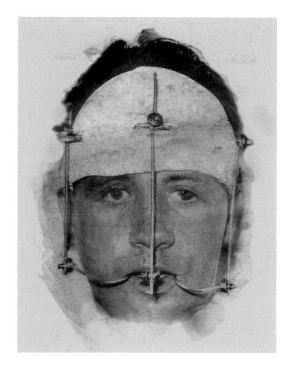

Rebuilding my face and after.

on his way to the hospital each day. Another six months of care followed with many demanding tasks for Pat who, among other things, had to feed me with liquid food through a tube as my new mouth was wired to a plaster head cast. During this time Alan Livingstone would drive both Pat and me to North Berwick where he would position me on the sandy beach, looking out to my favourite views of the Bass Rock and the island of Fidra. It was at North Berwick that I made my full recovery.

Before I could talk, I had been asked an unexpected question by the crash investigators. They had found that the Sutton harness (the retaining straps that secured me to the seat) had been cleanly cut through as if a knife had been used. This had enabled me to be ejected from the seat and had saved my life as the engine had been forced back towards the seat on impact. Had I been able to speak, I could not have given an answer to their questions. Later, I could only utter my own amazement to them. It would have been impossible to have cut through that tough harness while hurtling towards the ground. The report described this circumstance as 'supernatural'.

At the end of it I made a complete recovery but was to find that certain parts of my life were to become completely erased from my memory, never to return. However, several medicals later, I managed to get a reduced category to fly again and the very first aircraft I took up was a Tiger Moth. But this time it was a Tiger of *metal* construction. It was marvellous to be back in the air. I had pulled through; I had survived.

Our son Murray was born in Edinburgh in 1954. Hardly surprising, I was up in the air when the phone call came to tell me that Pat needed a Caesarean and could I sign the consent form. Just when it was my turn to be at her side and to look after her, Pat had to sign it herself!

Chapter 13

RAF Habbaniya

1955–58

For two years I had been off work recovering from my crash though I was able to do local flights to help myself get back to normal. But what I really needed to make a full recovery was a good dose of sunshine. The powers that be must have read my thoughts because in 1955 they made my next posting a camp set in an oasis in the middle of the desert. It was RAF Habbaniya near Baghdad, Iraq.

The station had two airfields, a lower one with the station buildings and a plateau strip, a single runway, which was 500 feet higher and a mile out from the station. The lower airfield was used by the Iraqi Air Force then being trained by RAF pilots to fly Vampires; the plateau was the runway for transit aircraft. My job was as a ferry pilot flying the station Pembroke, a twin-engine, eight-seater, light passenger, on runs to and from Baghdad using, of course, the plateau. Occasionally I would also take the Valletta to Nicosia, Cyprus. This was a Vickers twin-engined military transport plane. A particular memory of the runway is the time when a storm would hit and the ball lightning would run down the plateau towards us. Unpredictable and terrifying as it was, we would be sent diving for shelter.

I was fascinated by the way this station thrived in its oasis in the middle of a scorching desert. It was quite incredible. The base had been constructed in the 1930s on the west bank of the Euphrates, the main river running through Baghdad, which meant it could be irrigated by means of trenches and sluice gates. This was done so successfully that it could support a beautiful botanical garden, the Command Gardens, in the middle of the station. This was an ideal spot in which to sit out of the midday heat (often 120 degrees Fahrenheit (49°C)), to enjoy its coolness and admire its beauty. There was also the swimming pool, in fact there were two: one large enough for the airmen and their families and a second, smaller one kept for officers – our quarters were only a hundred yards away from this and very handy it was too! Pat and son Murray, then only two years old, had eventually come out to join me after a year on the waiting list. They threw themselves into the pool daily. Murray, fearless of the water and with water wings strapped to his back, would surprise everyone by doing running horizontal dives into the water. It reminded me of the dive I used to make when playing scrum half and passing the ball to the fly half from the scrum. We had several heart-in-the-mouth moments from his daredevil antics, including one where he climbed up to the high diving board and, with everyone shouting at him to come down, decided to jump off. On another occasion, he went hell for leather on one of his running flat dives

Murray performing his famous horizontal dive.

before we had had time to put his water wings on. At that moment I was on the far side of the pool getting coffee when I heard warning shouts that Murray was in the pool, wingless. I dropped the cups and did a running dive myself and brought him up, spluttering and surprised, but he was soon running about, with wings on this time, as if nothing had happened.

The civilians lived in the 'CC', the Civilian Cantonment which was a sort of village at the side of the station. It had a street called Cheapside and was aptly named, as one of the best buys I have ever made was done there: a Contax camera with an f1 Sonnar lens. It was a brilliant piece of apparatus which I was to use frequently on my cycle rides out to the nearby villages and the desert to take photographs of the locals. I took many, including some of the young shepherds herding their sheep along the dusty roads, and the results with the Contax were really good. When they were printed, the pictures reminded me of the illustrations in our family Bible back at home.

Close to the camp was Lake Habbaniya itself. This was huge, large enough for a Sunderland Flying Boat to take off and land. Seeing one lying at anchor on one visit, I wished I had watched it touch down; I missed its take-off, too. That would have been an interesting sight as it occurred to me that the lake was so calm the pilot would have needed a speedboat to break it up to help the second step of getting airborne. I was also left wondering just how much of that huge lake the Sunderland would have needed.

On one occasion that I was at the lake, King Faisal II was waterskiing behind his speedboat and thoroughly enjoying himself. His servants and bodyguards were in close attendance at the lakeside but did not restrict us, so that we were able to wait and watch the young king come in to land. In fact, he would often talk to us. It seemed he liked to talk to RAF personnel. After we had been posted home, the news of his assassination during the revolution in 1958 came as a shock.

There were some days when I would hire a taxi from the CC. The taxi would take the three of us out of the camp to Baghdad. Coming along too would be our bearer Turki, a young man of about eighteen who was to prove indispensable in so

Young shepherds outside Habbaniya, banks of the Euphrates.

many ways and in whom we had complete confidence when it came to looking after Murray. He was also able to translate for us and so we would have opportunities to shop without worry. The souk, or open-air market, was the most interesting of all the places. This was located down a dirty, dusty alley which we would not have entered without Turki but its stalls on both sides, laden with all kinds of exciting wares, would grab our attention instantly. In particular, the gold stall was a marvel to us, a real sight to behold, its pure-gold bracelets, its many rings and pots glittering in the shafts of sunlight that pierced the alleyway like searchlight beams. We learned that the worldly wealth of the nomadic desert Arabs was bought in the form of bracelets and their womenfolk wore them around their ankles, out of sight.

Further down the alley the pungent smell from the braziers of copper- and silversmiths would hit us, their blue smoke filling the air and mingling with the sound of constant hammering. Every now and then a cry that sounded something like 'bailck, bailck!' would come from behind. This, we soon learned, meant 'get out of the way!', and what was trying to get through would usually be a laden donkey. On one occasion we bought a large copper tray (which I still have) and knew we would have no difficulty fitting it into the boot of the taxi – taxis out there being mostly big American cars like Chevrolets and Buicks. It would come as a huge relief to get inside them and enjoy the comfort of their air conditioning.

Returning to camp, however, was not without its problems. We would have to pass through a border post at Fallujah. This was run by the Iraqi military. We were not stopped on the way into Baghdad but on one occasion on leaving the city we found the traffic at a standstill. The reason, we soon discovered, was that they wanted to give us a jab. We dismissed this most fervently by proving we were RAF. Poor Turki, however, was not so lucky. Hygiene was unheard of and the dirty syringe was used from one to the other in the line.

One trip I would like very much to have made was on the transit system between Baghdad and Amman in Jordan, on the 'Nairn flyer', the first stop down being Habbaniya. This was a huge bus with six-foot wheels each side of a bullet-shaped cabin. It was fully air-conditioned and extremely comfortable as the suspension was so sophisticated it had a gliding effect across the rough desert terrain. It was used mostly by the oil workers as the route followed the pipeline across the desert and stopped at various station halts along that line. This was one occasion when I regretted that all my trips to Amman were by air.

Returning to our married quarters from trips out was always a pleasure. Ours was an extremely comfortable bungalow in Palm Grove. It had a large living room and two bedrooms. The kitchen was at the rear and completely separate, joined by a passageway which was meshed against flies and mosquitoes. This was Turki's domain as he did all the cooking as well as the housework. It was largely thanks to him that our stay in that quarter was such a happy one, as in addition to all his other tasks he would often look after Murray without asking. At the end of each day he would walk home to his village, returning at first light the following morning. One morning, however, Turki did not arrive. I was visited by a member of his village to inform me that he had been arrested for manslaughter by their local sheikh and was in the main Baghdad prison. I got permission from the CO to visit him to try and find out what was going on. I flew into Baghdad that same morning and quickly found the prison – it was not a place I would forget in a hurry. I found myself in a very large hall with a bare wooden floor and a police sergeant sitting at a desk to one side. After a long discussion with him and then with various higher-ranked officers, I managed eventually to get them to agree for me to see Turki. I followed the sergeant across the hall to what seemed like a trapdoor in the floor. He bent to open it and I peered down to see four men huddled together in the darkness. One of them was Turki. He was almost pulled out by his hair and when he emerged he was shivering, and not from the cold of the pit. He was petrified.

I managed to prove to them that, as our servant, it would have been impossible for him to have been at the place where the alleged crime was supposed to have been committed, as he was with us in the house. Perhaps my RAF uniform, wings and medals helped. They let him go, and I was overjoyed to have him back and happy again in Palm Grove.

Going out at night was not recommended, so we did not do a great deal of socialising in the evenings. Walking along the verandas and walkways ran the risk of meeting a camel spider which would sit up on its hind legs and hiss, or coming across one of the many small poisonous snakes that seemed to be abundant there. There were also packs of pye dogs that would howl and rush around. The Arabs used the trick of removing their sandals and placing them flat on the ground with the toes pointing towards the howling pack. We tried it too and it seemed to work. The dogs stopped frequenting our area after that. But there was one particular occasion that stays in the memory, when we did venture out at night. The station officers had been invited by the sheikh from Ramadi to a 'coosie' or banquet. Turki would stay the night to take care of Murray. We got a taxi and, sharing it with several other officers, set off to Ramadi where we found a tremendous gathering of sheikhs from all around. We were ushered into a very large marquee with seats around its perimeter. There were no Arab females present, so our wives felt quite privileged to be at such an event but had to sit next to their husbands. A custom was that all talking must reach an end before the eating could start and as time rolled on and stomachs rumbled painfully, we were all desperately hoping that the conversation between the sheikhs would finish and we could get to the food. Eventually, we did. In came the servants with huge platters, carrying, among other things, a whole sheep, followed by smaller dishes with poultry. These were placed on tables in the middle and we all moved towards them with a plate. Hunks of sheep and chicken had to be torn off with the fingers, so I soon realised why the finger bowls were evident. Pat was in her element and seemed to delve her hand into the sheep with great delight regardless of the white fat that I had to avoid. But we did face one tricky moment when offered the delicacy of sheep's eyes. Our throats clamped at the thought. We managed to make our humble excuses by saying that it would be far better for the sheikh to enjoy them than ourselves. Fortunately, he agreed and promptly swallowed them with great gusto, followed by an equally enthusiastic burp. A good night was had by all.

As pleasurable as it was to have the family with me, there was work to be done. I flew the Pembroke to and from Baghdad many times accompanied by a navigator, Flt Lt Woods (nicknamed Timber), and sometimes we would go further afield to places such as Bahrain, Basrah and Kuwait. But the Pembroke's main function was to ferry the station commander to his various appointments. Group Captain Hughie Edwards, VC was an Australian and a law unto himself. His leg had been badly injured after a flying accident in 1938, but that had not prevented him from distinguishing himself as a brilliant pilot and leader during the war. Awarded the DSO and DFC, his VC was won leading a daring raid in 1941 of twelve Blenheims, flying at not much over fifty feet towards the heavily defended German port of Bremen.

More often than not, the Group Captain's appointments would be in Baghdad. Here he would have to attend meetings concerning the Baghdad Pact which was then being thrashed out. This was an organisation founded by Turkey, Iraq, Great Britain, Pakistan and Iran: its aim, to keep the communists at bay and maintain peace in the Middle East. It was impossible to know how long these meetings would take, which meant I would have to park the aircraft until they had finished. The sun would be scorching and the temperature in the cockpit could be as high as 160 degrees Fahrenheit (71°C). When it was time for me to climb in and switch on, I had to wear my flying gloves before I could touch the appropriate switches and to wear trousers to shield my legs from the burning seats. With the engines running, the air conditioning would cool the cabin and cockpit soon enough to a reasonable temperature. When possible, I would park under a raffia (straw) cover.

Other trips included a hospital run to Baghdad for the station doctor. This was at night. Flying from the plateau on a night trip meant using paraffin goose-neck flares for illumination of the runway. Unfortunately, paraffin was like gold dust to the nomadic desert Arabs and it was quite common to suddenly see flares go out. When air traffic got to them to relight them, they would find them missing. It was the practice that when a night flight was programmed, the flares would not be lit until the aircraft was on the return. One particular night flight involved the commanding officer. The conference had ended late and it was just about to get dark when he entered the cabin and came up to the cockpit, saying he would fly the aircraft back to 'Habb' himself. This was no problem. Timber moved out to the cabin and I moved over to the right-hand seat. The CO settled to do the checks and commence the flight. We took off and set course for Habb and all was well. The stars were bright, the night beautiful, and we looked forward to a nice, smooth flight back. But our pleasure was marred some-what on our approach to the plateau runway. Groupie was not happy. It seemed to him that the goose-neck flares were not bright enough. I noticed then that he was still wearing his sun-glasses but did not feel able to tell him! The landing was a bit hairy, to say the least.

We returned from RAF Habbaniya in 1958. I was sent to Little Rissington, to a desk job. It was not my most favourite kind of work; I wanted desperately to be in the air. Nor was it comfortable. After the desert, Britain seemed bitterly cold. As our quarters had only a single stove in the kitchen, I got per-mission to go out and buy some electric storage heaters. It was a far cry from Habbaniya!

Chapter 14

IRIS 1962

It was in the early Sixties that a wonderful opportunity presented itself for me to tour the Far East. I was attached to RAF Medmenham (Signals) in Buckinghamshire to join the IRIS team. This was the Inspectorate of Radio Services and Installations, a newly formed unit after the war whose job it was to supervise all RAF air traffic control and radio communications around the world.

I was informed that IRIS 2 had been taken ill and that I would be replacing him for the Far East tour. His task was to enunciate correctly and to speak clearly the messages transmitted from IRIS to the air traffic control of each station visited. As I was a qualified pilot on Hastings I would have the extra task of flying as second pilot to the captain, Flight Lieutenant Tom Stone.

I made my way from RAF Benson and reported for duty. Group Captain Griffiths-Jones, the officer commanding IRIS, explained the tasks I would be expected to carry out. The team was made up of the officers, Iris 1, 2, 3, 4, and the technicians whose job it was to check the radio installations and high-powered transmitter beams. There were also riggers and fitters. We all duly assembled at RAF Benson to board the Hastings and prepare for take-off.

The first leg of our flight was to Malta. I had not been back to the island since my wartime experiences there. My arrival the second time round was to be a much more civilised affair. When we were about 100 or 200 miles from the island I left the cockpit where I had been acting as second pilot and made my way to the main cabin, taking on the role of IRIS 2 and calling up Luqa air traffic control to check the range and clarity of their reply. I continued with these checks until we were in close range, when I left the main cabin and returned to the cockpit to assist in the landing procedure. Once the landing was complete, I took off my flying overalls and returned to the main cabin to accompany the IRIS team to meet the waiting station officers. This was to become my routine procedure at every station visited.

The second leg was from Luqa to El Adem in Libya and was a short flight requiring only that I act as second pilot. The third, from El Adem to Kormaksa, Aden, was a seven-hour flight, so we halved the flying time. Trouble in Ethiopia meant we had had to amend our route, flying inland over Sudan and Kenya until we reached the Indian Ocean, then turning up the coast of Somalia and on to Aden.

I completed my checks and we landed at Kormaksa, an extremely hot and humid place that made our shirts stick to our backs and stay that way throughout the visit. We were put up in a hotel in the town and transported to the aerodrome to complete our checks. When these were done we were taken back to the hotel and had time to explore the town.

The fourth leg of the trip was from Aden to RAF Gan. In the middle of the Indian Ocean, Gan is the most southerly island of the Maldives. Originally a Royal Navy base built in the early part of the war it was transferred to the Royal Air Force in the Fifties and used as a stopover for the Far East Air Force in Singapore. The trip from Aden to Gan was to be another long one, a flight of ten hours this time – five hours' flying for both of us. Always on long flights we would engage the autopilot (George) which helped. Again, with my usual checks completed, we landed at Gan, at an aerodrome made up of a runway and a few station buildings built on the coral. Under the coral was an encatchment to store rainwater, the main water supply for the station. We were met by the CO and his staff. The IRIS team set to work. One of its tasks was to inspect the long-range transmitter out on another island, Hithadhoo. To get to it meant a trip on a high-speed boat.

The Hithadhoo transmitter had a range of 1,000 miles and was used by both military and civil aircraft as well as by ships crossing the oceans. It was vital to keep it in first-class condition and serviceable at all times. I personally had no checks to carry out, so my visit to it was purely out of interest and the desire to ride on a high-speed launch, which was Gan's air-sea rescue launch. The trip was not without its dangers, though! We had been advised not to stand too close to the edge of the deck: the ultraviolet rays from the sun would reflect from the white bow wake of the boat and on to our uncovered knees and arms, resulting in severe sunburn. The team completed their checks (these usually lasted about two days) and we returned to base.

The station on Gan provided some interesting distractions for our leisure time, one of which was to snorkel over the coral reef close to the shore. The seawater was warm and clear, the bright tropical fish seemingly fearless in passing us by, our feet flapping heavily in plimsolls to protect them from the sharp coral. Another treat, one evening this time, was the rare privilege of watching a ritual dance by the native islanders. This was the 'Fish Dance', a sacred ritual in recognition of the fact that the island depended for its existence on fishing. The dance was not unlike the more familiar Dragon Dance: a long line of men covered, caterpillar-like, with palm leaves, a giant fish head at one end. It was performed with great enthusiasm and was appreciated by all. The speed and agility of these islanders was quite amazing, and shown to great effect by the native boys who held races to see who could be the first to climb up a palm tree and cut off two coconuts to fall to the ground, all done with bare feet and hands.

Gan had been my first experience of a tropical island and was a pleasant surprise. We had crossed the equator and for the first time in my life I had been able to see in the clear night sky one of the most distinctive constellations in the southern hemisphere, the Southern Cross. With novelties such as this, and with its beauty, colour and climate I did think, for one brief moment, what a wonderful posting it might be. But there was one major disadvantage. This was primarily an air traffic control, not a flying, post. I knew that a few months here and I would be bored.

Our next stop, the fifth leg, was Changi, Singapore. At Gan, I had begun to feel I was on a 'jolly', but there was plenty of work to be got through. The flight to Singapore was another ten-hour trip, and again we shared the time on the control column. As we approached the Malacca Straits, we were confronted by a solid wall of cumulonimbus, the most dangerous kind of cloud to fly into. Its up-and-down currents of air can lift the aircraft up or down 1,000 feet, a quite alarming sensation when holding a specific height to clear a mountain range, for instance. Not only that, but a lightning strike on an aircraft in cloud can be extremely unnerving. It was my turn at the stick as it happened, but Tom the captain was also in the cockpit consulting with the navigator to see if we could fly down the length of this cloud and find a gap to fly through. The navigator agreed but said that we would have to turn left on course before long, regardless of the 'cu-nim'. No gap appeared and I had to turn left. We entered it and then began the inevitable, the battle with the elements that threw the Hastings about like a leaf. I had already warned all the passengers in the main cabin to 'belt up', disengaged George which could not have coped with this kind of flying, and after a full half-hour of being tossed about requested that Tom assist me. He agreed, and together we battled with the stick, which made things easier. This was an experience that made me feel even more thankful that I had managed to become proficient with instrument-flying.

Eventually we did break cloud. Our navigator had been spot on; we were flying down the Malacca Straits. Thank goodness, too, because on our left was the Malaysia peninsula and, on our right, Sumatra suffering at the time under a terrific storm of almost continuous lightning flashes. This was a trip I would not forget in a hurry. It was with some relief that we approached Changi in smooth flight and I was able to hand over to Tom and get on with my r/t checks with Changi control. We landed and following the usual procedure, which by now was routine, were met and escorted to our quarters for the stay.

During my checks I visited the control tower and was surprised to find that, to enter it, I had to bend forward to lower myself sufficiently in order to walk without bumping my head on the ceiling. The Japanese had built and occupied the tower during the war and had obviously made it to suit their smaller stature.

On our free day, I made my way to Changi village and was amazed at how cheap everything was; the temptation to keep buying was great. I managed to restrict myself to getting a few toys for Murray, one of which was a battery-operated speed-boat. For Pat, I bought a complete set of Noritake chinaware, the finest, most delicate bone china. We also had time to visit the Singapore swimming club where on Sundays it appeared the local boys held water polo matches followed by a curry. The dishes were laid out on tables the length of one side of the pool. It was quite a sight – and quite a taste, too. I have never had a better one since. Again, the life of the men in Signals Command began to look extremely appealing, but I was only too aware of my own good fortune to have been selected for the job and to be flying the Hastings.

From then on Changi was to be our base from which we were to make the subsequent trips in the region, the first of which was to Kai Tak, Hong Kong. This was to be a long, nine-and-a-half-hour flight. We took off from Changi, headed up the South China Sea, passing Borneo on our right and over the northern tip of the Philippines. The navigator requested that he be told of any ships sailing below so that he could take a bearing and plot their position and approximate speed at that time. He explained that if we were to get into any difficulty and had to ditch, he would head our aircraft towards the nearest ship. I thought this was marvellous. To have a navigator work out an emergency plan seemed like the height of luxury. After all, as a fighter pilot I had never had the privilege of a navigator's skill.

Having rounded the tip of the Philippines, we flew over the Gulf of Tonkin with Vietnam on our left, and headed up the coast to Kai Tak. When we were abeam of the islands that lie north of Kowloon we turned left to pick up the Changzhou beacon. Flying on this would take us over the many islands below and in sight of the 'Checkerboard'. As its name suggests, this was a black-and-white-squared marking painted on the hillside to guide pilots into Kai Tak. On reaching this we then had to turn right ninety degrees, which meant a very steep, almost vertical bank to get on to the runway heading. Straightening up, we then commenced a five-degree glide path to reach the threshold of the runway. This was a very steep descent which rather alarmed passengers who had been used to normal, shallow approaches for landing. The glide path passed extremely close over Kowloon just before reaching the threshold and the flare-out that followed was almost like pulling out of a dive; all very interesting for us pilots and crew but not so for the passengers. At least it gave them something to talk about! There were actually two approaches to Kai Tak. The one we took was the most used as its heading was towards the sea, the prevailing wind coming in from it. The other, heading from the sea, used the Wagland beacon and was for ILS (Instrument Landing System) approaches in bad weather with light wind.

I had completed my r/t checks before crossing the islands but for the rest of the team there were many more to do. I asked if I could accompany them to the radar installation on Lion Mountain, a large radar dome behind Hong Kong. On the journey up there, we were to discover that it was not just the flying approach to the country that was hairy. The local drivers thought nothing of going at fifty miles an hour up winding mountain roads and cutting the corners on the wrong side. It was a miracle we arrived safely at the radar site.

But we did and the technicians set to work. I watched with fascination and asked a lot of questions which they readily answered. I noticed that part of the radar screen had been blanked off. This was, of course, blanking the coverage of the Chinese air space. No doubt they would have had a quick peak if ever there had been any trouble!

Back at the station and in our free time I went with a few others from the team into Kowloon and, again, was struck by how cheap the things were in the shops and markets. We ate at a Chinese restaurant and, unsure of what I was getting, had to trust to my companions' better knowledge and hope that whatever arrived on my plate would not make me sick. Our departure from Kai Tak was a gentle one, taking off towards the sea with a steady climb, course set back to Changi and a seven-and-a-half-hour flight, sharing the flying time.

A short flight to Labuan, North Borneo was to be the seventh leg with me flying as second pilot. We headed up the South China Sea for three and a half hours to reach the north coast and the landing strip at Labuan, in Brunei. Here my services in carrying out r/t checks were not required. I had understood this to be a listening post – and secret. This fact was highlighted when we landed. I accompanied the team to the CO's office, an outpost in the jungle where, to our amusement, he talked to the lizards that climbed his office walls. I was left behind in the office while he accompanied the team further into the jungle. It occurred to me that, to pass the time, I might try my hand at communicating with the little reptiles. They clearly did not find me as companionable as the CO. They gave me a short, sharp stare and disappeared like a flash. With the return of the team, we made our way back to the landing strip, boarded the Hastings and prepared for take-off. We were not to return immediately to Changi this time but to call at Butterworth on the Malaysian peninsula, flying round and past Singapore, a flight of only five and a half hours.

Butterworth faced the Malacca Straits and was an Australian station. When I did the r/t and range checks with air traffic control, I could barely keep a serious voice when a strong Australian accent replied, 'G'day, Blue, I am hearing you OK.' Listening in as always to all transmissions, the Iris Group Captain nearly had a fit. His expectation was for correct r/t procedures to be adhered to at all times. This Antipodean laxness was guaranteed to raise his blood pressure. He had to accept, however, that there was little he could do other than speak to the CO on landing and, eventually, he calmed down. Again, there was not much for me to do here but I did go up to the control tower and had a cup of tea with a very burly Australian controller. I said nothing about his r/t greeting! Later I joined our captain, Tom Stone, and we made our way down to the waterfront intending to go for a swim or a paddle, only to be told by the locals not to, as it was infested with sea snakes. We were glad to head back to Changi, relieved to have just a two-and-a-half-hour flight down the Malacca Straits with no thunderstorm in sight. We engaged George and relaxed. It had been a tedious day with two stations to visit.

I have no memories of the next trip, our tenth – none at all. The amnesia that would strike randomly after my severe crash in the Tiger Moth took this episode as one of its casualties. I can only give details from the entry written in my logbook. The flight was a long eleven hours, so as usual we shared the flying times. On landing, it was noted that, inconveniently, a tall palm tree was situated in the middle of the take-off path. This, Tom pointed out, would give us some difficulty when taking off with a heavy load and insisted that, when the IRIS team was ready to depart, take-off in the Hastings would have to be very early in the morning in order to clear the tree – around 5.30 a.m. in fact. It was a very disgruntled Group Captain who emerged from bed at 3.00 a.m. Nevertheless, the tree was cleared successfully and the course set for Kormaksa once more. We returned eventually to England following the same route we had taken on the outward journey. Of course, the British weather had to give us its traditional welcome when we finally reached our homeland; we were diverted from RAF Benson to Lyneham. But this was a mere insignificance in a marvellous trip I will never forget.

Chapter 15

Final Farewell

I left the RAF in 1976 at the age of fifty-five. It had been a wonderful career, a wonderful life. Adjusting to the civilian world was not easy; I found it unreal and that people were not as straightforward, not as direct as in the service. There was also the question of finding a job. My age was against me. Every job I applied for I was told I was too old even after attending an interview for the post of pilot on the Thames.

Finally, at fifty-six and desperate to get work, I went to Wimpey the builders to become a salesman for their houses. I thought the link to architecture I had had before the war might be of use but I need not have worried. The sales manager told me he was not bothered by my age, he was looking to take on ex-military. In the end, I became a very successful salesman. As I already had my RAF pension I did not have to fight for every bit of commission, which would have meant using the hard-sell tactics of my colleagues. With the pressure off, clients were more inclined to come back and buy.

I last piloted a plane at the age of seventy. It was a Tiger Moth. We took off from Rednal, Shropshire and the owner very kindly let me take control. He was also happy for me to land it but was somewhat alarmed when I put it into a quick side-slip. Fearing that he was seeing the last of his beautiful aircraft and, possibly too, the last of this world, he was mightily relieved when I brought the plane level and landed it gently on the runway. This was a manoeuvre I had, of course, used many times in a Tiger Moth and one he had never tried. He and I have often recalled that flight since, with much amusement.

Many, many years have passed since the heady days of the war and the years following it. Many different circumstances have taken lives in various directions but some things have come full circle.

In 2010 we heard from Dessie. She was living in the south of England and had rung to tell us that, sadly, Johnnie Meyer, my close friend and comrade in the baling-out exercise at Gravesend, had died. My dear wife Pat was herself taken ill in the autumn of that same year. She had looked after me when I had suffered that awful crash, now it was my turn to look after her. Caring for Pat was very tiring but worth it. Sadly, she died in May 2012.

A memory of Pat while I was PMC at RAF Binbrook.

Others from my past have also been in touch: Joyce, still living in Scotland, and my driver from Turnhouse, Alan Livingstone, who after the war had set up a turfing business with his wife Betty in Musselburgh near Edinburgh.

Speaking with such voices from the past has had the effect of shrinking the years, bringing memories of those early, intense times vividly back to life and, with them, the thrilling sense of youth and adventure.

* * * * *

It is amazing to me, reading back through these chapters, how much I did survive and it makes me appreciate life all the more. What I need to do now is to survive old age which I find most difficult to accept! I don't recommend it to anyone but it comes to most of us – eventually.